1000 FACTS ON
WORLD WAR I

First published by Bardfield Press in 2006
Copyright © Miles Kelly Publishing Ltd 2006

Bardfield Press is an imprint of
Miles Kelly Publishing Ltd
Bardfield Centre, Great Bardfield, Essex, CM7 4SL

2 4 6 8 10 9 7 5 3 1

Editorial Director: Belinda Gallagher
Art Director: Jo Brewer
Copy Editor: John Furniss
Assistant Editor and Picture Researcher: Amanda Askew
Designer: Stephan Davis
Image Department Manager: Liberty Newton
Reprographics: Anthony Cambray, Mike Coupe, Stephan Davis, Ian Paulyn
Indexer: Jane Parker

British Library Cataloguing-in-Publication Data
A catalogue record for this book is available from the British Library

ISBN 1-84236-677-7

Printed in China

www.mileskelly.net
info@mileskelly.net

1000 FACTS ON
WORLD WAR I

Rupert Matthews
Consultant: Brian Williams

BARDFIELD
PRESS

Contents

Contents

1917: THE WAR SPREADS

1918: THE WAR TO END ALL WARS

A Europe of empires

- **Before 1914**, Europe was dominated by three large empires that no longer exist today – the German Empire, the Russian Empire and the Habsburg Empire, which is sometimes called Austria-Hungary.

- **A fourth empire** was the Turkish-Ottoman Empire, which once ruled all of southeastern Europe, but by 1914, only ruled the Middle East.

- **All of these empires** were governed by dictators who took little notice of democracy or the wishes of their peoples.

- **The German Empire** included modern Germany and parts of what are now France, Poland, Denmark and the Czech Republic. It was the newest empire, founded in 1871 when the smaller German states joined together.

- **The Russian Empire** included modern Russia, plus Latvia, Estonia, Lithuania, Finland, Ukraine, Belorussia, Turkmenistan, Kazakhstan, Uzbekistan, Tajikistan, Kirghizistan and part of Poland.

- **The Habsburg Empire** included modern Austria, Hungary, Serbia, Montenegro, Croatia, Slovenia, Slovakia and parts of the Czech Republic, Poland, Italy and Romania.

- **There were several smaller independent countries**, such as Switzerland, Belgium, the Netherlands and the Scandinavian countries. In the Balkans were several new countries that had become independent in the previous 50 years as the Turkish-Ottoman Empire broke up.

- **Some European countries**, such as Britain, France and Germany, ruled extensive overseas empires in Africa, Asia and the Pacific.

- **There was great inequality** of wealth in Europe. Some countries, such as Britain and those in the German Empire, were rich and prosperous with advanced industrial activity. Other countries, such as those in the Russian Empire and Bulgaria, were poor, with few factories or good roads.

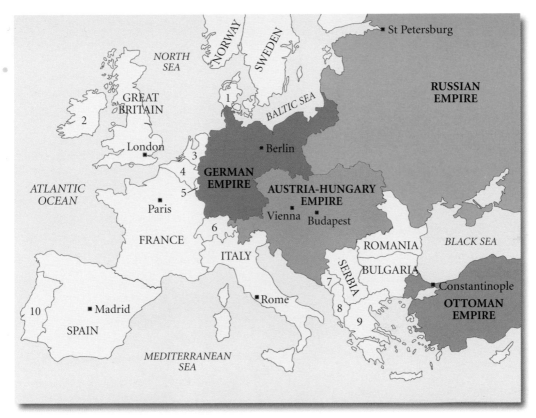

KEY

1 Denmark	6 Switzerland
2 Ireland	7 Montenegro
3 Netherlands	8 Albania
4 Belgium	9 Greece
5 Luxembourg	10 Portugal

▲ *Europe in 1914. The empires of Germany and Austria-Hungary dominated central Europe, while Russia and the Ottoman Empire stood to the east. France and Britain were dominant in the west.*

. . . **FASCINATING FACT** . . .
Some countries in Europe were republics, such as France, but most were monarchies, which had a king or emperor as head of state.

The alliances

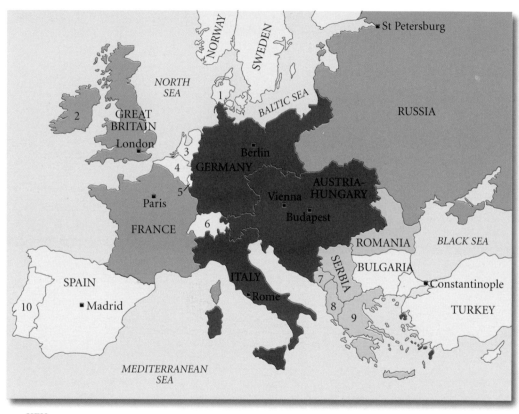

KEY

■ Triple Alliance/Central Powers	4 Belgium
■ Triple Entente/Allies	5 Luxembourg
□ Neutral	6 Switzerland
■ Balkan League	7 Montenegro
1 Denmark	8 Albania
2 Ireland	9 Greece
3 Netherlands	10 Portugal

▲ *In the early years of the 20th century many countries sought security by forming alliances with other countries. These alliances proved to be particularly crucial in World War I.*

- **For almost 100 years**, Europe had been peaceful. The foreign ministers and diplomats of the different countries met regularly to discuss problems and opportunities. They were usually able to reach a compromise without a war.

- **Since 1815**, there had only been two major wars, and both of these were over quickly. The Crimean War of 1854 set the Ottomans, Britain and France against Russia in a dispute over the Balkans.

- **The other conflict**, the wars of German reunification, saw the German states fight Austria and France and unite to form the German Empire.

- **Even when a war did take place**, the diplomats ensured that the results were reasonable. Neither side fought to destroy the other, but simply to ensure they got their way in a particular dispute.

- **Countries formed alliances** to support each other if a particular event were to occur. Some lasted a short period of time, others for many years.

- **In 1887**, Spain and Italy signed a ten-year treaty agreeing to join their navies together if either were attacked by France. This agreement was designed to counter the power of the growing French Mediterranean fleet.

- **In 1897**, the Habsburg Empire signed a ten-year treaty with Russia promising to block any changes in the Balkans. The small Balkan countries had many disputes with each other, but Russia and Austria preferred peace and stability, rather than letting the Balkan states sort things out by force.

- **By 1914**, Germany and Austria were linked by the Triple Alliance with Italy.

- **At the same time**, Russia and France were tied into a similar alliance.

- **Britain was linked to France** and Russia by various agreements, but had not signed a firm alliance. However, Britain was allied to Belgium and promised to help if any other country tried to invade it.

Great power rivalries

- **In the years before World War I** there were numerous incidents and clashes between the great powers. Each of these was eventually solved by diplomats without a war. However, each incident led to increased tension and mistrust.

- **On 12 June 1900,** Germany announced a 17-year plan to construct the second largest navy in the world. Britain, which had the largest, was worried that Germany might try to use the new navy to attack its empire.

- **In 1904,** Britain began an even larger programme of building warships. It started with the battleship, *Dreadnought*.

- **The First Moroccan Crisis** of 1905 began when France tried to force the Sultan of Morocco to sign a trade treaty. This would have given France control of the country. Germany objected. A conference was held in Spain at Algeciras in April 1906, where a compromise was reached.

- **In October 1908,** Austria announced that it was taking over the provinces of Bosnia and Herzegovina from the Ottomans. Austria had been running the area for 30 years, giving the excuse that it was protecting the Christian inhabitants from the Muslim Turks.

- **Serbia and Montenegro** objected to the takeover of Bosnia and Herzegovina. Russia backed the Serbs, while Germany supported the Austrians. In 1909, a compromise was reached that saw Austria buy the provinces legally from the Ottomans.

- **In July 1911,** the Second Moroccan Crisis began when the German warship, *Panther*, steamed into the port of Agadir. The Kaiser complained about the French treatment of Germans in Morocco. After a tense few weeks, Germany accepted a compromise.

- **On 27 August 1911**, Kaiser Wilhelm II made a famous speech saying that Germany wanted 'a place in the sun', meaning he wanted Germany to be recognized as an important power by other countries. He made it clear that Germany would not back down again in a future crisis.

- **On 29 September 1911**, Italy demanded that the Ottomans allow Italian merchants in Tripoli greater freedom. The Ottomans offered a compromise, but Italy invaded Tripoli anyway.

- **After a short war**, the Ottomans gave up all of Libya to Italy. The Balkan countries realized the Ottomans were very weak.

▶ *The German ruler, Kaiser Wilhelm II, wanted Germany to gain the power and prestige that he believed it was entitled to.*

The Balkan Wars

- **The Balkans lie between the Black**, Adriatic and Aegean seas. In 1912 it was made up of Serbia, Bulgaria, Greece, Romania and Montenegro. Both the Ottoman and Austrian empires ruled large areas of the Balkans.

- **All the smaller countries** in the Balkans had previously been part of the Ottoman Empire. They wanted to help those Christian people still living under Muslim Ottoman rule to become free as well.

- **The Austrian Empire was concerned** that various countries in the Balkans wanted to become independent. Austria opposed the expansion of the small Balkan states, especially Serbia, which was the most powerful of them all.

- **The Russian Empire exported grain** and other goods by ship through the straits at Constantinople. This was extremely profitable, thus it was vital that Russia maintained good relationships with whoever controlled these straits.

- **The Ottoman Empire was weak** and poor. The Turks wanted to keep control of the lands they still held, while they carried out reforms of their government and economic systems.

▶ *In 1912 the small Balkan nations joined together to capture land from the Ottoman Empire.*

- **On 8 October 1912**, the tiny country of Montenegro invaded the Ottoman Empire. Within 10 days, Bulgaria, Serbia and Greece had joined the war on Montenegro's side. The Ottoman army was defeated within a few months.

- **In May 1913**, Russia, Austria, Britain and France organized a peace conference. In the Treaty of London, Bulgaria, Montenegro, Serbia and Greece were each given parts of the Ottoman Empire, which was reduced to the area around Constantinople. A new country, Albania, was created.

- **On 29 June 1913**, Bulgaria was attacked by Greece, Serbia and Romania. Bulgaria had to give up the areas it gained under the Treaty of London.

- **Austria was furious** that the small countries had grown in size and wealth so quickly. It was particularly worried about Serbia because many Serbs lived in the Habsburg Empire and may leave to join the independent kingdom of Serbia. The Austrians decided to teach Serbia a lesson.

- **After the two Balkan wars**, every country in the Balkans had a dispute with another at some time.

▶ *By 1913 the Balkan nations had defeated the Ottomans, but now argued with each other over how to divide their conquests.*

On the brink of war

- **The summer of 1914** was long, warm and peaceful. All the recent international crises had been resolved without fighting, and the small wars in the Balkans were over. The world economy was booming. Most people looked forward to a prosperous and peaceful future.

- **However, international tensions** were high. Germany wanted power and prosperity. Austria was determined to restrain Serbia's growth. Russia was suffering internal social unrest, so the Tsar wanted a foreign success. Each had decided not to back down in a future crisis.

- **France had an army** of 3.5 million men and a navy with 28 battleships and 28 cruisers. It earned about £425 million in trade and had a population of 40 million.

- **Germany could field an army** of 8.5 million men and had a navy of 40 battleships and 57 cruisers. The German Empire made about £1 billion in trade in 1913 and had a population of 65 million.

- **Russia could field an army** of 4.4 million men, with another 10 million in reserve, and a navy of 16 battleships and 14 cruisers. The Russian Empire earned £190 million in trade and had a population of 167 million.

- **The Austrian Empire had an army** of 3 million men and a navy of 16 battleships and 12 cruisers. The empire earned £198 million in trade and had a population of 49 million.

- **Britain had an army** of 711,000 and a navy of 64 battleships and 121 cruisers. It earned £1.2 billion in trade and had a population of 46 million.

- **Turkey had an army** of 360,000 men and a small navy with no battleships or cruisers. It earned £67 million in trade and had a population of 21 million.

- **Most army officers in all countries expected** that if a war did break out, it would be fought in a similar fashion to wars in the 19th century. Cavalry would act as scouts, artillery would shell fortified positions and infantry would fight the main battles with rifles.

- **Everybody expected that a war would be over** very quickly. It was thought that there would be one or two big battles, then the loser would offer to make peace, compromising on the original dispute.

▶ *Charge of the Light Brigade, 25 October 1854. The Crimean War (1854–1856) was fought in traditional style. If a war were to break out in 1914, most generals expected it to be fought in the same way.*

Murder in Sarajevo

- **In June 1914**, the Austrian army was due to undertake manoeuvres in the southern part of the Habsburg Empire near Sarajevo, the capital of Bosnia.

- **Archduke Franz Ferdinand**, the heir to Austrian Emperor Franz Josef, was to review the troops and supervise the action.

- **A few days before the manoeuvres** took place, it was decided that Archduke Franz Ferdinand would also visit leading citizens in Sarajevo. They wished to discuss a proposal, which would give the area self-government.

- **Three Serb extremists were planning** to murder the Archduke. They belonged to the Black Hand terrorist organization.

- **Black Hand was led** by Vojislav Tankosic, a citizen of Serbia. He received weapons, money and information from Colonel Dragutin Apis, who served on the General Staff of Serbia.

- **When Franz Ferdinand arrived** in Sarajevo, he got into a car and drove to his meeting as part of a convoy. Black Hand activists, Nedeljko Cabrinovic, Gavrilo Princip and Andri Grabez, were waiting to murder him.

- **As the cars left the railway station**, Cabrinovic threw a hand grenade. He missed the cars, but about 20 civilians and an army officer were injured.

◀ *Police seize Gravilo Princip after his first attempt to assassinate the Archduke.*

- **After the meeting**, the convoy drove back through Sarajevo. Princip pulled a gun, but was grabbed by a policeman. He freed himself and opened fire.

- **The first bullet killed the duchess**, the second injured an army officer and the third hit the Archduke in the neck. He died less than ten minutes later. Princip was arrested.

- **Although Vojislav Tankosic planned the murder** of Archduke Franz Ferdinand, he stayed safely in Serbia himself.

▶ *The Archduke and his wife prepare to climb into their car just minutes before they were both shot dead.*

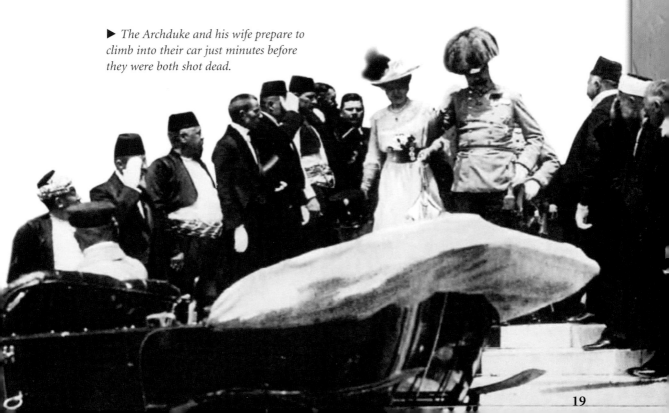

The war begins

- **After the assassination** of Archduke Franz Ferdinand, the Austrians quickly discovered that the killer, Gavrilo Princip, was a member of the Black Hand terrorist group. They knew Black Hand was supported by Serbia's army and thought Serbia had planned the murder.

- **Austrian Emperor Franz Josef** and his government decided to use the murder as a reason to crush Serbia. They began to prepare for war, but sent army commander Count Conrad von Hötzendorf on holiday to make it appear that they did not expect war.

- **Kaiser Wilhelm II of Germany** promised to support Austria, but King Victor Emmanuel III of Italy refused. He said Italy would only join Austria if Serbia attacked first.

- **Serbia contacted its ally**, Russia. Tsar Nicholas II advised Serbia to call a conference if Austria began a war. The Tsar then ordered part of the Russian army to march towards the Austrian frontier to act as a threat.

- **Russia contacted its ally**, France, to ask for support. The French government said it would only join a war if Russia were attacked, but not if Russia attacked Austria first.

- **On 23 July**, the Austrian government announced the results of their inquiry into the murder of the Archduke. They demanded that the Serb government ban anti-Austrian organizations and newspapers, sack a number of government officials, arrest Tankosic, head of the Black Hand terrorist group, and open a judicial inquiry with an Austrian judge in charge.

- **On 25 July**, Serbia agreed to all the demands, but said the inquiry should have a Serb judge. The German, Russian and French governments thought this was reasonable and believed that war had been avoided.

▶ *On 3 August 1914 the* Daily Sketch *carried reports on the mood of the British public as war began to seem more likely.*

- **On 28 July**, Austria turned down the Serb offer and declared war. They sent a telegram to the Serb government. This was the first time that war had been declared by telegram, instead of by a meeting between the two sides.

- **At first**, Serb Prime Minister Sibe Milicic thought it was a joke, believing that a government would not declare war by telegram. Then a second telegram arrived from a frontier post to say that Austrian artillery had opened fire.

- **The war had begun** at 3 p.m. on 28 July 1914.

The Schlieffen Plan

- **As the Austrian army marched** into Serbia, the Serbs appealed to Russia for help. Tsar Nicholas II decided to send the Russian army to the Austrian frontier, then demand talks with Austria to agree a peace deal in Serbia.

- **The Russian generals told the Tsar** that if the army marched on Austria, Russia would be helpless against Germany. On 29 July 1914, the Tsar agreed to mobilize all Russia's reserves.

- **On 30 July**, Kaiser Wilhelm II ordered Germany to mobilize for war. He informed Russia that unless they demobilized, Germany would declare war.

- **Russia informed its ally**, France, of the German message. On 31 July, France began to mobilize for war.

- **Tsar Nicholas refused** to stand down the Russian army. Germany and Austria declared war on Russia on 1 August.

- **On 1 August**, Kaiser Wilhelm ordered General Helmuth von Moltke to implement the Schlieffen Plan. It detailed troop movements and how supplies would be organized.

▼ *A German regiment advances in open order across a field in northern France. In the early weeks of the war there was much movement in the open.*

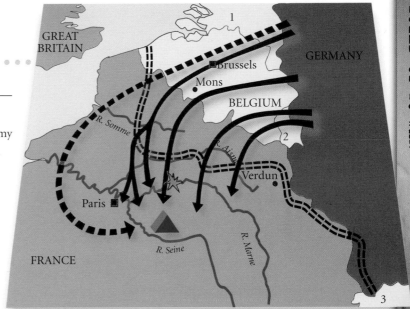

KEY

✳ Battle of the Marne

▄▄▄► Intended route of German army

▬► Actual route of German army

▲ British and French armies

▬▬▬ Western Front trenches

1 Netherlands
2 Luxembourg
3 Switzerland

▲ *The Schlieffen Plan. The Germans began the war with an attack on France that involved marching through Belgium. This plan, named the Schlieffen Plan after General von Schlieffen who invented it, went wrong, as the French and British resistance was tougher than expected.*

- **The plan involved** defeating France before Russia could mobilize its reserves.

- **The Schlieffen Plan put small forces** on the Russian border and in fortified positions on the French border. The main German armies would then march through Belgium to capture Paris and force France to surrender. Then the German armies would be moved east to defeat Russia.

- **On 3 August**, Germany declared war on France. The German ambassador in Brussels asked the Belgian government to allow German troops to march across Belgium into France.

- **On 4 August**, Belgium refused. Germany declared war on Belgium. Britain (Belgium's ally) declared war on Germany.

'Brave Little Belgium'

- **By noon on 4 August 1914**, the main German armies were marching into Belgium. This was the same day that Britain declared war on Germany.

- **The Belgians had fortified** the town of Liége with six forts containing a network of gun positions, held by General Gérard Leman and 22,000 men.

- **The Liége forts held out** until 15 August, when German General von Emmich brought up heavy siege mortars. The new guns fired shells weighing almost one tonne and smashed the Belgian forts.

- **When German soldiers entered the Liége forts**, they found Leman senseless and badly wounded, and took him prisoner. When Leman came to, he asked Emmich, "Please put in your despatch that I was unconscious and did not surrender." Emmich did as requested.

- **The German advance into Belgium** was swift. Many Belgian reservists did not have time to get their uniforms. They began cutting telephone wires and ambushing German supply wagons while still wearing civilian clothes.

- **The Germans declared** that it was against the rules of war for civilians to attack soldiers. In reprisal they executed dozens of hostages and burned the city of Louvain.

> ### FASCINATING FACT
> British and French newspapers exaggerated the stories of German reprisals in Belgium. They printed drawings of German soldiers bayonetting women and babies.

▲ *These Belgian soldiers wear straw in their hats as camouflage so they are not seen by German riflemen.*

- **The Belgian army continued** to fight. Soon Belgium became known as 'Brave Little Belgium' for standing up to the mighty German army.

- **Meanwhile, the French had invaded** Germany at Sarrebourg and Morhange. They soon occupied most of the territory they had lost to Germany in 1871.

- **Britain began sending troops** to France on the way to help Belgium. One of the first to arrive was Lieutenant R N Vaughan of the Royal Flying Corps who landed his aircraft at Boulogne on 13 August. He was immediately arrested by the French who thought he was an Austrian spy.

Retreat from Mons

▼ *British newspapers conjured up the spirits of previous generations of British soldiers to raise morale.*

- **On 21 August**, the British Expeditionary Force arrived in the Belgian town of Mons. The force consisted of two corps, formations made up of several divisions, commanded by General Sir John French. They also had the French army on their right.

- **Kaiser Wilhelm II ordered** General von Moltke to "push aside that contemptible little army." When the British soldiers learned of this, they began calling themselves 'Old Contemptibles'.

- **On 23 August**, the Germans attacked at Mons. The British were trained in defensive warfare and rapid rifle fire, and inflicted heavy casualties.

- **The French suffered** very heavy casualties and that night they retreated. This left the British isolated, so French ordered his men to fall back towards Paris. The retreat from Mons had begun.

- **On 24 August**, a German aircraft observing the British retreat was shot down by a British artillery shell near Le Quesnoy. This was the first time an aircraft was shot down in a war.

- **A day later**, Moltke sent troops from Belgium to reinforce the troops facing Russia. This seriously weakened the German attack.

- **The British halted** at Le Cateau on 26 August and managed to drive off numerous German attacks. The delay enabled many units to escape capture.

- **On 27 August**, a force of British troops became lost and by nightfall was surrounded by Germans.

- **Just after midnight** they saw a woman carrying a lantern. She pointed towards a road that led to safety. The British soldiers said she was an angel.

- **Within days the story** of the 'Angel of Mons' was known throughout the British army. The story was printed in newspapers across the world.

Miracle on the Marne

- **On 1 September 1914**, General von Moltke ordered his advance units to swing east of Paris to cut off the French army, instead of capturing the city. It was the second change he had made to the Schlieffen Plan.

- **At noon on 2 September**, a French airman saw the columns of German troops marching away from Paris. He landed and reported to General Joseph Gallieni, commander of the garrison in Paris. Gallieni sent a message to the commander in chief, General Joseph Joffre.

- **Gallieni then sent messages** to all French units near Paris asking them to come to the city. Most responded, even if they were not under his command.

- **On 5 September**, Joffre met General Sir John French to ask the British to join the French army in attacking the Germans at the river Marne. Joffre hit the table with his fist and shouted, "Monsieur, the honour of England is at stake." French blushed and said, "I will do all that is possible."

- **Gallieni's troops were named** the 6th Army and ordered to attack. But there were not enough trains or trucks to carry the men. In desperation, Gallieni hired every taxi in Paris to take the men forward.

- **German General von Kluck** moved his men north to attack Paris on 7 September. This opened a gap between his men and those of German General von Bülow to the east.

> ### FASCINATING FACT
> The German VII Corps marched over 60 km in 24 hours to close the gap and halt the British advance.

- **On 8 September**, Joffre asked General Foch, commanding the French centre, what was happening. Foch replied, "My left is in retreat. My centre is yielding. My right is giving way. Situation excellent, I attack tomorrow."

- **On 9 September**, the British found no German troops in front of them. They marched quickly through the gap between Kluck and Bülow, cutting the German army in two.

- **On 14 September**, the German armies began to retreat all along the line. The Schlieffen Plan had failed. The French called these events 'The Miracle on the Marne'.

▶ *British infantry sleep in the open before digging in on the river Marne.*

The Battle of the Aisne

Russia

USA

Britain

Japan

- **After the defeat on the river Marne**, German commander in chief Helmuth von Moltke ordered his armies to retreat to the river Aisne.

- **When they reached the Aisne**, the Germans took up position on the hills north of the river. From there they could shoot accurately at any troops trying to cross the river.

- **British and French pilots scouting** the German positions found they were often shot at by soldiers of their own armies. They began painting red, white and blue stripes on the wings of their aircraft.

- **A few weeks later, the High Command** ordered the pilots to paint standard markings on their aircraft. British planes had a red circle inside a white circle inside a blue circle. French aircraft sported the same circles in reverse.

- **The German pilots also began** painting a black cross on their aircraft.

◀ *Aircraft markings. By 1915, the pilots of each nation were painting symbols on their aircraft to help identify friend from foe. The Allies chose round symbols, the Central Powers chose crosses.*

- **On 13 September 1914,** the British, together with the French 5th and 6th Armies, crossed the river Aisne on pontoon bridges under heavy fire and attacked the Germans. They broke the German lines and moved forwards.

- **The following day** the British and French found themselves faced by German troops in trenches and machine gun nests. Unable to advance against heavy fire, nor to inflict casualties on the Germans, the allies halted and dug their own trenches.

- **General Joffre ordered** a new attack on 18 September, but his men failed to make any advance and suffered heavy casualties. Joffre called off the attack and ordered his artillery to begin shelling the German trenches.

- **The Battle of the Aisne** marked the beginning of trench warfare on the Western Front.

- **Kaiser Wilhelm II sacked** General von Moltke as commander in chief and replaced him with General Erich von Falkenhayn.

Belgium

France

Germany

Bulgaria

31

The Battle of Tannenberg

- **On the Eastern Front** in 1914, the Russians fought the Austrians and the Germans. The key strategic factor was that Russian Poland extended far to the west, separating most of the Austrian Empire from German Prussia.

- **The Central Powers** – Germany and Austria – planned to remain on the defensive until France had been defeated. This was known as Plan R.

- **Russian generals had devised** a defensive Plan G and an offensive Plan A. Tsar Nicholas decided to adopt Plan A, sending two armies to invade East Prussia. At dawn on 12 August the Russian 1st Army invaded from the east while the 2nd Army invaded from the south.

▼ *Russian invasion. The Russian attack on East Prussia began well, but an outflanking move by the Germans isolated and crushed the southern Russian army at Tannenberg.*

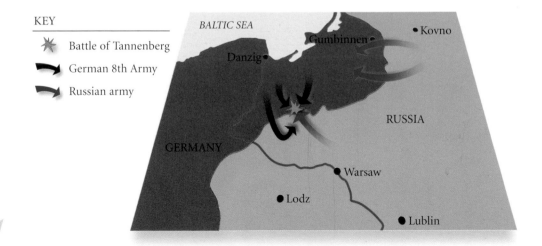

KEY

✳ Battle of Tannenberg

➤ German 8th Army

➤ Russian army

BALTIC SEA

• Kovno

Gumbinnen •

Danzig •

RUSSIA

GERMANY

• Warsaw

• Lodz

• Lublin

- **On 17 August**, the Russian 1st Army led by General Rennenkampf met the German 8th Army under General von Prittwitz. After three days of fighting, the Germans fell back in confusion.

- **On 20 August**, the Russian 1st Army captured Gumbinnen. Kaiser Wilhelm II sacked the defeated Prittwitz and replaced him with General von Hindenburg.

- **When he took command** in East Prussia, Hindenburg was already 67 years old and had retired four years earlier. He had not fought in a war for over 40 years.

- **Hindenburg decided to abandon** much of East Prussia to the Russian 1st Army. He moved his men south to face General Samsonov's 2nd Army. He had enough men to outnumber Samsonov.

- **On 28 August**, the Germans outflanked the Russians' left wing and attacked from the rear at Tannenberg.

- **The Russians fled south**, but were hemmed in by marshes and swamps. Of 200,000 Russians, about 30,000 were killed and 90,000 captured. Samsonov committed suicide rather than surrender.

- **After the Battle of Tannenberg**, Hindenburg moved his force northeast by rail to attack the Russian 1st Army near the Masurian Lakes. Rennenkampf retreated rather than risk defeat.

▶ *A German infantry soldier of 1915. A smooth helmet that is better suited to trench warfare has replaced the old spiked version. Puttees are worn around the legs to withstand the mud.*

From Lemberg to Lodz

- **The Russian Plan A involved** an attack on the Austrian Empire as soon as enough troops had been mobilized. The attack began on 17 August 1914.

- **The Russian 4th Army** under General Ivanov attacked near Lublin, supported by the 3rd and 8th Armies under General Brusilov. The Austrian 2nd and 3rd Armies fell back slowly. On 30 August, the Russians captured Lemberg (now Lvov).

- **On 4 September**, the Austrians launched a large-scale attack on the Russian centre. It failed, and the Austrian retreat soon became disorderly as the supply system collapsed and soldiers fled.

- **By 20 September**, the Austrians had lost 110,000 men killed or wounded and 220,000 men captured. Another 100,000 men were cut off at Przemysl. The Russians were advancing quickly through Galicia towards the vital German industrial area of Silesia.

- **The German commander in the east**, Hindenburg, took two-thirds of his men from East Prussia and formed them into the 9th Army, to protect Silesia.

◀ *A German Luger 9 mm automatic pistol. Officers carried pistols that were useful for close fighting, but were small enough not to interfere with their command responsibilities.*

▲ *At the Eastern Front, a unit of the Austro-Hungarian army rests as a column of German infantry march past them on their way to the Eastern Front.*

- **On 6 October**, the German 9th Army attacked, but the Russians threatened to cut off the advancing troops, so Hindenburg called off the attack.

- **In early November**, the Germans overheard a Russian general talking to his officers by radio. They learned that the Russians would attack Silesia on 14 November in the area around Lodz.

- **Hindenburg put the 9th Army** under General Mackensen with orders to attack first, on 11 November.

- **Mackensen's attack** went well. On 16 November the Germans broke through the Russian lines and surrounded some Russian units, inflicting heavy casualties on others.

- **Tsar Nicholas II sacked** General Rennenkampf and appointed a new commander, General Litvinov. His first orders were for the entire Russian army to retreat to the river Bzura.

Race for the sea

- **The commander of the French armies** as the Battle of the Aisne ended was General Joffre. He was quiet, patient and believed that the Germans could be defeated by 'nibbling' – taking small advantages when he could.

- **Joffre was so old-fashioned** that he refused to use the telephone. Instead a junior officer spoke on the phone and passed on messages.

- **The British commander**, General Sir John French, was a cavalryman who believed in swift movement and decisions. He hated working with Joffre.

- **Most of the Belgian army** was trapped in and around Antwerp. On 6 October, the army began retreating towards Calais.

- **Having captured Antwerp**, the Germans hoped to capture the ports of Calais, Boulogne and Dunkirk through which Britain was sending supplies to France.

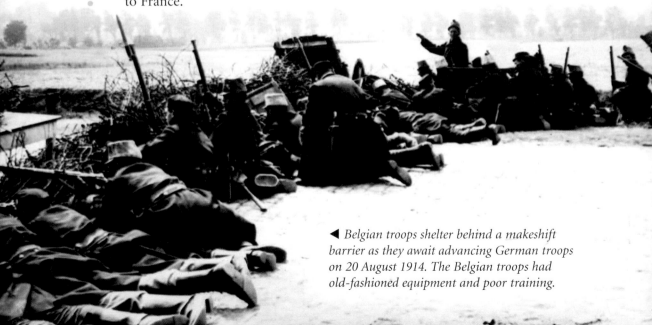

◀ *Belgian troops shelter behind a makeshift barrier as they await advancing German troops on 20 August 1914. The Belgian troops had old-fashioned equipment and poor training.*

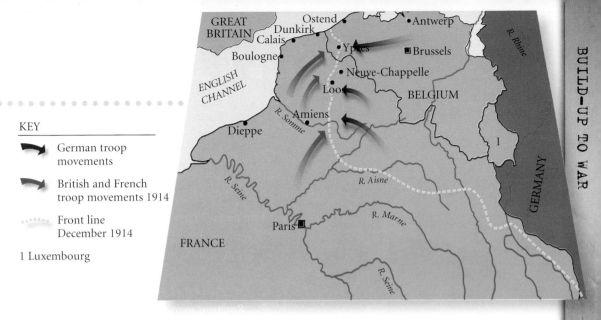

KEY

➤ German troop
movements

➤ British and French
troop movements 1914

···· Front line
December 1914

1 Luxembourg

▲ *Once the first German attack on Paris had been defeated, the opposing forces launched a series of outflanking moves that carried the area to the north. By September a front line had been established between the English Channel and Switzerland.*

- **On 6 October,** a fresh British division arrived in France and was driven to the front in London buses. The German attack was halted.

- **The Germans moved south,** reaching Lille on 11 October. They shelled the city heavily. On 13 October the city, now largely rubble, surrendered.

- **German troops from the river Aisne** were marching north hoping to outflank the French. However, the French were too fast and tried to outflank the Germans.

- **In a final attempt to outflank** the Germans, Joffre asked French to move to a certain small town – it was to play a huge part in the oncoming war and as such, its name became famous – Ypres.

- **The British arrived on 15 October,** only to find the Germans marching in from the east. A savage battle broke out around the town.

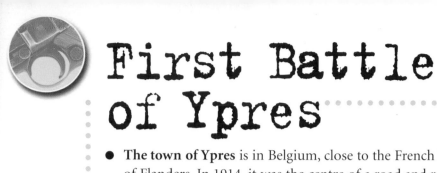

First Battle of Ypres

- **The town of Ypres** is in Belgium, close to the French border in the province of Flanders. In 1914, it was the centre of a road and rail network and a vital transportation centre for the British and French armies.

- **The name 'Ypres'** is actually pronounced 'weep-ers', but the British soldiers came to know it as 'wipers'.

◄ Men of the Royal Warwickshire Regiment were transported to Ypres on London buses, commandeered by the army.

> **...FASCINATING FACT...**
> The bars in Ypres served a cheap white wine called vin blanc,
> pronounced 'van blonck' by the locals. British soldiers called it 'plonk',
> which came to mean cheap, easily obtainable alcohol.

- **On 21 October**, the Germans attacked the British around Ypres. General Erich von Falkenhayn was confident of success so he invited the Kaiser to watch the battle, and lead the victory parade.

- **As at Mons**, the German attack ran into the highly trained soldiers of the British army. Their rapid, accurate rifle fire inflicted heavy losses, but the Germans had overwhelming numbers and heavy artillery.

- **On 31 October**, the Germans broke through the British front line, then through the rear line at Gheluvelt. General Sir John French knew he had no reserves left. There was nothing to stop the Germans. He wrote later 'It was the most nerve-shattering time of my life'.

- **However, Brigadier General Fitzclarence** then remembered that 368 men of the 2nd Battalion Worcestershire Regiment were recovering from severe fighting south of Ypres. He ordered them to march to Chateau Gheluvelt.

- **The 2nd Battalion attacked** the 244th Saxon Regiment that was leading the Germans. They reached Gheluvelt and were at once assaulted by the 242nd and 245th Saxon Regiments. At sunset the German attacks ceased, by which time only 140 of the 2nd Battalion were still standing.

- **At 7 p.m. Fitzclarence sent a message** to French that read 'My line holds'.

- **The next day**, the Kaiser returned to Berlin. The First Battle of Ypres dragged on until 11 November, but the Germans did not break through.

The Christmas truce

- **By December 1914**, a dense network of trenches stretched from the English Channel to the Swiss border. The trenches were damp, cold and very dangerous places to live.

- **The weather in December** was dreadful with heavy rain and cold winds. The trenches filled with water and the earth walls collapsed in many places.

- **On 21 December**, things began to change. The weather became dry, sunny and cold. Soldiers on both sides stopped fighting while they repaired their trenches, dried their clothes and tried to make themselves more comfortable.

- **King George V of Britain sent** a Christmas card to every soldier fighting in France. His daughter, the popular Princess Mary, sent a small box of sweets to each man on active duty.

- **On the German side**, the Kaiser sent a cigar to each soldier. The German army made sure that every regiment received a Christmas tree and lanterns.

- **On Christmas Eve**, the German soldiers in the front line lit their lanterns, put up their Christmas trees and sang Christmas carols. The British joined in with the English carols that had the same tunes.

- **At dawn on Christmas Day** a sergeant in the 133rd Saxon Regiment who had worked in Birmingham before the war, waved a Christmas tree above the trench and called to the British soldiers opposite, "Happy Christmas." He then climbed out of the trench and was met by a British captain.

> **. . . FASCINATING FACT . . .**
> The trenches of the opposing armies were surprisingly close,
> in places only 20 m apart.

Friday, January 8, 1915

The Daily Mirror

CERTIFIED CIRCULATION LARGER THAN ANY OTHER DAILY NEWSPAPER IN THE WORLD

WHY DELAY? THE DAILY MIRROR OVERSEAS WEEKLY EDITION contains all the Latest and Best War Pictures and News, and is therefore the Best Weekly Newspaper for your friends abroad. You can obtain it from your Newsagent for 3d. per copy. Subscription rates (prepaid) post free, to Canada for six months 10s.; elsewhere abroad 15s. Address—Manager, "Overseas Daily Mirror," 23-29, Bouverie Street, London, E.C.

AN HISTORIC GROUP: BRITISH AND GERMAN SOLDIERS PHOTOGRAPHED TOGETHER.

▲ *A group of German and British soldiers photographed between their trenches on Christmas Day.*

- **All along the front line** similar scenes took place. By lunchtime the opposing armies were meeting in peace. Men used the time to bury the dead, then they swapped souvenirs and in at least one place, the Germans and English played football.

- **In most areas the war began** again on Boxing Day, or soon after. In a few places along the front line, intense warfare never started up again and they became known as 'quiet sectors'. The largest of these was at the Bois de Ploegsteert, called 'Plugstreet Wood' by the British. It was still quiet in 1918.

41

The trenches

- **In the winter of 1914–15** the soldiers on the Western Front believed that the trenches were only temporary structures. They thought that when good spring weather arrived, the armies would return to traditional fighting tactics.

- **The trenches were based on temporary** field defences that all armies built when stationary for a few days. They were designed to shelter men from artillery shells and rifle bullets.

▼ *The trenches were reinforced with timber supports to make them stronger.*

- **Trenches were designed** to be over 2.3 m deep, so that men could walk along them without needing to crouch.

- **A firing step was built** into the front of the trench. Standing on this, a man could aim his rifle over the top towards the enemy. Sentries stood on the firing step to see if the enemy were attacking.

- **Trenches were built in zig-zag routes** so that there was no straight stretch of more than 30 m. This meant that nobody could aim a gun along the trench to kill everyone in it.

- **In 1914**, there were usually two or three lines of trenches. The front trench contained most of the men, ready to repel an enemy attack. The second and third trenches contained essential services.

- **The different lines of trenches** were linked by communication trenches that ran forwards. They were quite shallow and did not have firing steps.

- **In marshy areas or rainy weather**, the trenches often filled with water very quickly. Hand-powered pumps were installed to keep the trenches dry, but they did not work very effectively.

- **Sandbags and wooden planks** were used to give strength and shape to the trench walls. Collapsing trenches were a problem throughout winter.

- **Barbed wire was strung on metal posts** in front of the trenches to slow down attacking soldiers, so that the defenders had more time to shoot them.

▶ *Barbed wire was placed around trenches to hinder and slow down oncoming attacks.*

43

Life on the front line

- **Infantry soldiers in the trenches** had an uncomfortable life during the winter of 1914–15.

- **Each battalion stayed on the front line** for a few days, then it moved to form a reserve close to the front line. Then it would be moved to the rear so that the men could rest before going back to the front line again.

- **Battalions** changed position at night, moving along communication trenches. Units stayed in the same area for months, so they knew the trenches well.

- **Trenches were infested** with lice, fleas and other vermin. The British soldiers called these creatures 'chats'. Each day men went to the second or third trench to pick the vermin off each other. This was called 'going for a chat'.

- **Soldiers began to suffer** from a new disease called 'trench foot'. It was caused when feet were wet and cold for more than 48 hours at a time. The feet became infected with fungus. It was so painful, men could not stand.

- **In January**, February and March 1915, more than 30,000 British soldiers got trench foot. They had to be taken out of the fighting to go barefoot in warm, dry houses for two weeks to cure the condition.

- **In April 1915**, it was found that trench foot could be prevented if boots were made waterproof by soaking them in whale oil and socks were changed three times each day. By 1916 trench foot was a rare disease.

> ### FASCINATING FACT
> Boredom was a major problem. The soldiers formed choirs, drama groups and trench schools to help pass the time.

- **Soldiers tried** to make themselves feel at home by giving familiar names to the trenches. London soldiers called trenches names such as 'Regent Street'.

- **It was often too dangerous** to retrieve bodies of men who were killed. The bodies lay rotting in the open for weeks.

▼ *A British officer inspects the feet of his men for signs of the disease, trench foot, which could cripple a man.*

The evening hate

▼ Gas balloons carried men equipped with maps and radio sets who identified enemy targets for the artillery.

- **Although no major attacks** were launched through the winter of 1914–15, the armies remained at war.

- **Both sides chose their best shots** to act as snipers. These men watched the enemy trenches and shot at anyone they saw moving.

- **At night, patrols of men** crept forward from the front trench. They repaired the barbed wire, spied on the enemy and sometimes slipped into the enemy trench to kill the sentries.

- **Even when no major battle** was taking place, the front line was a dangerous place. About one in every 500 men was killed or badly wounded every day.

- **Artillery placed hundreds of metres** behind the trenches would fire shells at the enemy throughout the day. They would aim at trenches, or at roads and railways behind the lines.

- **The artillery often opened fire** in the first few hours of darkness when enemy soldiers would be going on patrol, or moving from the front line to the reserves. This became known as 'the evening hate'.

- **Men began digging dugouts**, or underground rooms, which were safer than trenches against artillery fire.

- **During the day**, large balloons carrying men in baskets were flown. The men used telescopes to scout the ground behind enemy lines, then phoned messages to their artillery saying where to aim.

- **One British balloon scout** wore a top hat and purple velvet jacket. He became known as 'Burlington Bertie', from a famous song of the time.

- **Enemy balloons were shot down** with machine guns and light artillery. Whenever 'Burlington Bertie' had his balloon punctured he would step out of the basket and pretend to run in thin air, before opening his parachute.

The Battle of Neuve-Chappelle

- **In February 1915**, French commander in chief, Joseph Joffre, asked British commander, Sir John French, if he could attack in March. Joffre wanted the British to attack to divert the Germans from a larger French attack in April.

- **French chose to attack** the village of Neuve-Chappelle and Aubers Ridge. This would threaten the city of Lille.

▲ *Gurkhas, soldiers recruited from Nepal, carried a sharp kukri for close combat.*

- **The plan was to pound** the German trenches with artillery. Then the infantry would charge forwards to capture the trenches and break through. Finally the cavalry would attack German supply lines and reinforcements.

- **French hoped he could break out** of the trenches and once again return to traditional styles of fighting. The war, he hoped, would be over in a few weeks.

- **On 10 March**, 400 British field guns opened fire, smashing the German trenches and cutting the barbed wire. Nearly 50 battalions of British infantry charged forwards. Some took heavy casualties from machine guns, but most reached and captured the German trenches.

- **That night the British attacked** again. At Neuve-Chappelle the infantry broke through the German lines to reach open country. However, the messages sent back to bring up the cavalry failed to get through.

- **Similar attacks continued** for three weeks, but the British never managed to make a sustained breakthrough.

- **The troops attacking Neuve-Chappelle** included a regiment of Gurkhas. One Gurkha was the son of a nobleman and came equipped with a beautiful silver kukri, the curved knife used in close action by Gurkhas.

- **The Gurkha with the silver kukri** was part of a patrol. He slipped into a German trench and cut the throat of the sentry. Instead of returning, he then crept along the trench to kill the next sentry.

- **For weeks afterwards**, British patrols found German sentries with their throats cut. For three months the killing continued, then it stopped. Presumably the Gurkha had been killed.

▼ *British infantry attacking from their trenches went 'over the top' of the trench parapet to race forwards.*

Turkey invades Russia

▲ *The fighting between Russia and the Ottoman Empire took place to the southeast of the Black Sea. Each side invaded the other, but heavy losses and bad weather brought an early end to active campaigning.*

- **In 1911 and 1912,** the Ottoman Empire suffered humiliating defeats by Italy and the small Balkan kingdoms. The reforming Turkish government of Enver Pasha invited Germany to send military advisers to improve the Turkish army.

- **By 1914,** the Ottomans had about 360,000 men with modern equipment who had undergone German training. There were another 750,000 men in reserve who had not yet received the new weapons and training.

- **On 29 October 1914,** the Turks allowed two German cruisers through the straits at Constantinople to attack Russian ships and towns in the Black Sea.

- **In response to the Black Sea raid**, Russia invaded Turkey near Batum. Turkey declared war on Russia, and its allies Britain and France on 5 November 1914.

- **Turkey immediately banned** all shipping from using the straits at Constantinople. The waters were sown with mines and eight batteries of heavy guns were put into strong fortifications.

- **On 7 November**, a British-Indian force of 4500 men landed at Fao on the Persian Gulf. The army seized the port of Basra, but did not move inland. It was there to protect oil exports from Persia, modern Iran.

- **In January 1915**, the Turkish 3rd Army, commanded by Enver Pasha, crossed the Caucasus Mountains to invade Russia. After savage fighting, the Turks pulled back, but were caught by blizzards in the mountains. Only 12,000 out of 140,000 men got back to Turkey alive.

- **In February**, the Turkish 4th Army sent 20,000 men to attack the Suez Canal. The attack was driven back by a force of Australian, New Zealand and Indian troops from British-occupied Egypt.

- **In March**, Russia announced that its foreign exports had been cut by 95 percent since the Turks had closed the straits at Constantinople. This blow meant Russia might soon become bankrupt.

...FASCINATING FACT...

The Germans had also paid for and built railways in the Ottoman Empire. They also helped to modernize the economy, building new factories and advising on government laws and regulations.

Italy invades Austria

▼ *A parade through London organized by Czech nationalists living in the city. The Czechs resented their home country being ruled by Austria and supported the Italian entry into the war.*

THE LONDON CZECHS GREET ITALY AND HER ALLIES. DOWN WITH AUSTRIA

- **When war broke out** in 1914, Italy refused to join its allies Germany and Austria. Although Italy opposed the growth of French power in the Mediterranean, it had no real interest in the Balkans.

- **The alliance did not oblige** Italy to join Austria in an offensive war, but only to join if Austria were attacked. Italy remained neutral.

- **Many people in Italy resented** the fact that the Austrian Empire ruled Italian-speaking areas. They wanted them joined to Italy. These nationalists began to think Italy should invade Austria to seize the provinces.

- **Another group in Italy** supported the democracies of Britain and France against the imperial Germany and Austria. Italy was itself a democracy.

- **The democratic position was championed** by the newspaper *Avanti!,* which was edited by the journalist Benito Mussolini. In 1922, Mussolini would become the fascist dictator of Italy.

- **In February 1915**, Italian Prime Minister Antonio Salandra asked the Austrian government if they would give the Italian-speaking lands to Italy in return for Italy declaring war on France. The Austrians refused.

- **In March**, Salandra asked the French and British if they would give Italy the disputed areas in return for Italy declaring war on Austria – assuming that Austria lost the war. The British and French agreed.

- **On 24 May**, Italy declared war on Austria.

- **On 23 June**, 25 Italian divisions invaded the Austrian Empire at the river Isonzo, which was held by 14 Austrian divisions. The attack petered out after two weeks with no real gain.

- **By the end of 1915**, Italy had lost 66,000 killed, 185,000 wounded and 22,000 captured. Its troops had advanced only 5 km into Austria.

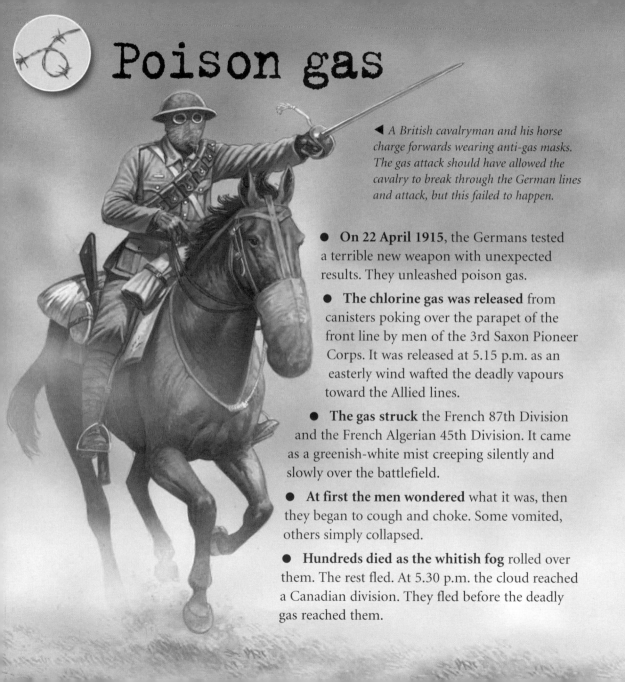

Poison gas

◄ *A British cavalryman and his horse charge forwards wearing anti-gas masks. The gas attack should have allowed the cavalry to break through the German lines and attack, but this failed to happen.*

● **On 22 April 1915**, the Germans tested a terrible new weapon with unexpected results. They unleashed poison gas.

● **The chlorine gas was released** from canisters poking over the parapet of the front line by men of the 3rd Saxon Pioneer Corps. It was released at 5.15 p.m. as an easterly wind wafted the deadly vapours toward the Allied lines.

● **The gas struck** the French 87th Division and the French Algerian 45th Division. It came as a greenish-white mist creeping silently and slowly over the battlefield.

● **At first the men wondered** what it was, then they began to cough and choke. Some vomited, others simply collapsed.

● **Hundreds died as the whitish fog** rolled over them. The rest fled. At 5.30 p.m. the cloud reached a Canadian division. They fled before the deadly gas reached them.

▶ *A pair of German engineers prepare to release poison gas from a canister through pipes leading out of the trench.*

- **At 5.40 p.m.** a senior British officer riding out of Ypres saw the French and Algerians running towards him in panic. He tried to question them, and managed to understand one officer who gasped, "The fog."

- **At 5.45 p.m.** a Canadian officer who had been a chemist before the war ordered his men to urinate into their handkerchiefs and hold them over their mouths. With these makeshift gas masks the Canadians manned two machine guns to await a German attack.

- **At 5.55 p.m.** the cloud of gas, by this time greatly dissipated, entered Ypres. Civilians were reduced to helplessness, but few died.

- **The gas worked by irritating** the lining of the lungs and throat, causing them to produce watery liquid. If enough gas was inhaled, the liquid gathered in the lungs and drowned the victim.

- **The Germans were unable to break through** the deserted trenches because the front line regiments had not been issued with gas masks. It was the best chance the Germans had of winning in the west, but they missed it.

Second Battle of Ypres

- **After the Battle of Neuve-Chappelle,** both sides ordered a halt to any fresh attack while the senior commanders studied what had happened.

- **The British believed** that they had found the answer to the trench deadlock. The combination of artillery, infantry and cavalry would win victory, but only if there was more artillery and a second attack to support the first.

- **All British infantry were now equipped** with metal helmets, which gave some protection against shell splinters and bullets.

- **The Germans recognized** that the British knew how to break a conventional front line of three trenches. They believed the answer was to build a second line of three trenches behind the first and put more machine guns on the front line.

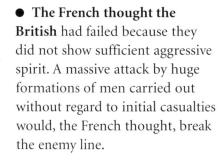

- **The French thought the British** had failed because they did not show sufficient aggressive spirit. A massive attack by huge formations of men carried out without regard to initial casualties would, the French thought, break the enemy line.

◀ *The heavy machine gun now dominated the battlefield and inflicted heavy casualties.*

- **On 9 May**, the British attacked from Ypres towards the Aubers Ridge. The attack was preceded by a heavy artillery barrage.

- **The British attack at Ypres** was met by the increased number of German machine guns. Casualties proved to be very heavy, but again messages failed to get back to headquarters.

- **The supporting attack was ordered** forward by officers who were unaware that the first attack had failed. The second formations also took very heavy casualties.

- **By 25 May**, the British had lost 60,000 men, the Germans 35,000 men. General Sir John French called off the attack. Again he and his staff studied the results.

- **General Sir Horace Smith-Dorrien protested** loudly that attacking Germans who were in trenches and armed with machine guns was suicidal and would only lead to massive British casualties. He was promptly sacked by the British government.

▶ *A British soldier of 1915. He has puttees wrapped around his legs for protection against mud and a steel helmet to give protection from shell splinters.*

57

Landings at Gallipoli

- **In January 1915**, the British government debated what to do about the straits at Constantinople, known as the Dardanelles. Since these had been closed by Turkey, Russia had been facing economic crisis.

- **Winston Churchill**, First Lord of the Admiralty, suggested sending a force of old battleships. He knew the guns guarding the straits were old and short of ammunition, but did not know of the underwater mines.

▼ *A British medium howitzer shells Turkish positions in Gallipoli. It took several days to get these large guns into action, by which time Turkish defences were well organized.*

- **On 19 March**, the British Mediterranean fleet attacked the Dardanelles. The first Turkish batteries were destroyed, but then mines sank three British battleships and damaged three more. Admiral Robeck called off the attack.

- **The troops on the British ships** intended to capture, then garrison the straits and city of Constantinople. It was now decided to use the troops to land on the Gallipoli peninsula and attack Constantinople by land.

- **General Sir Ian Hamilton refused** to land until he had more troops, which gave the German general commanding the Turkish troops, Liman von Sanders, time to prepare his defences.

- **British, Australian and New Zealand troops landed** on 25 April. There was little opposition, but Hamilton refused to allow his men to advance until scouts had been sent forward.

- **By the time the scouts returned**, a Turkish regiment had begun a furious counter attack, led by Colonel Mustapha Kemal, later to become president of Turkey.

- **By sunset on the first day**, the landings were in confusion and had advanced only one kilometre inland. Hamilton sent his reserves ashore to launch a new attack. The assault failed and by 8 May the invaders had lost 6000 killed and 14,000 wounded out of 70,000.

- **On 10 May**, Turkish torpedo boats sank three more British ships. The fleet withdrew. The troops on shore were alone.

The Battle of Gorlice-Tarnow

- **During the winter months**, Kaiser Wilhelm II and his commander in chief, Erich von Falkenhayn, had devised a new plan to win the war. They decided to crush Russia in 1915, then turn against France in 1916.

- **After the Battle of Neuve-Chappelle**, Falkenhayn believed his new double trench line could defeat any Allied attack in France. He could afford to move men, artillery and supplies to the Eastern Front.

- **During April**, the Germans built up a large force in Galicia, west of the river San, under the command of General Mackensen.

- **On 1 May,** the Germans fired 700,000 shells into the Russian forces between the towns of Gorlice and Tarnow. Then the massed German regiments poured forwards. The Russians in the front line threw down their rifles and fled.

- **In the first week** of the attack, Mackensen advanced over 120 km. Over 200,000 Russians had surrendered to the Germans.

- **In the second week**, Mackensen captured the city of Jaroslaw and crossed the river San. Two weeks later his men captured the fortress city of Przemysl.

- **Meanwhile, German General von Ludendorff** attacked the northern end of the Eastern Front from East Prussia. Rather than risk being outflanked by the southern attack, the Russians retreated.

▶ *A British .38 calibre Webley revolver. British infantry officers throughout the war carried these guns. The ring on the but (handle) was attached to a leather strap that was buckled to the man's belt.*

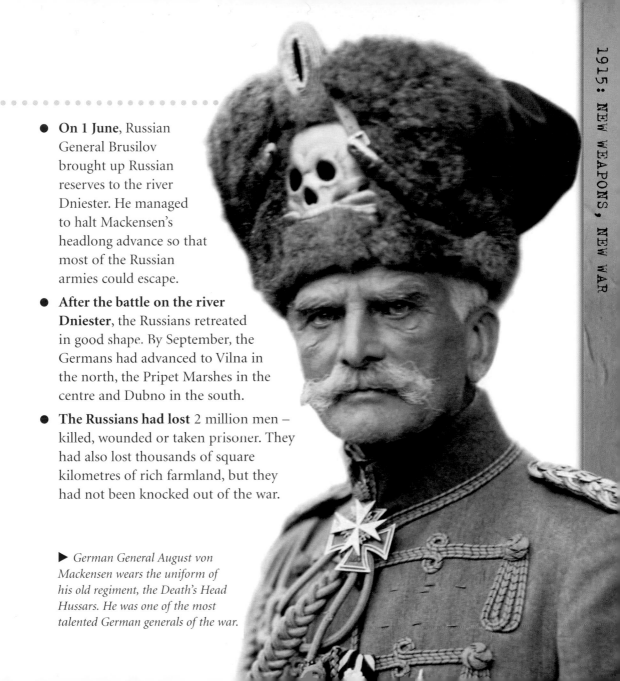

- **On 1 June**, Russian General Brusilov brought up Russian reserves to the river Dniester. He managed to halt Mackensen's headlong advance so that most of the Russian armies could escape.

- **After the battle on the river Dniester**, the Russians retreated in good shape. By September, the Germans had advanced to Vilna in the north, the Pripet Marshes in the centre and Dubno in the south.

- **The Russians had lost** 2 million men – killed, wounded or taken prisoner. They had also lost thousands of square kilometres of rich farmland, but they had not been knocked out of the war.

▶ *German General August von Mackensen wears the uniform of his old regiment, the Death's Head Hussars. He was one of the most talented German generals of the war.*

War in Africa

- **When the war broke out** in Europe, the Europeans living in other parts of the world were at war as well. In Africa there were numerous territories and colonies owned by the combatant nations. War flared up instantly.

- **Germany ruled Togoland** (now Togo), Cameroons (Camaroon), Southwest Africa (Namibia) and German East Africa (Tanzania).

- **Belgium ruled Congo** (now Democratic Republic of Congo).

- **France ruled French Congo** (Gabon), Algeria and French West Africa (Chad, Central African Republic, Niger, Burkina, Cote d'Ivoire, Guinea, Senegal, Mauritania, Mali and Benin).

- **Britain ruled South Africa**, Bechuanaland (Botswana), Rhodesia and Nyasaland (Zambia, Zimbabwe and Malawi), Uganda, Kenya, British Somaliland (part of Eritrea), Nigeria, Gold Coast (Ghana), Sierra Leone, Sudan and Egypt.

- **The British navy moved quickly** to cut off the German colonies from reinforcements or resupply. The Germans in the colonies were on their own.

- **Togoland was conquered** quickly by French forces for French West Africa. Southwest Africa was overrun by South African forces by July 1915. In 1915, Cameroons was conquered by French soldiers advancing from French Congo.

- **The strongest German force** was in German East Africa, with several hundred German soldiers, plus thousands of local troops.

- **The main Allied assault on German East Africa** began when the Royal Navy shelled Dar-es-Salaam in 1916. Meanwhile, British forces invaded from Kenya, South African forces from Rhodesia and a Belgian force from Congo.

- **German General Lettow-Vorbeck fell back**, ambushing his pursuers and raiding supply lines. He stayed in the Rufiji Valley until November 1918, when Germany surrendered.

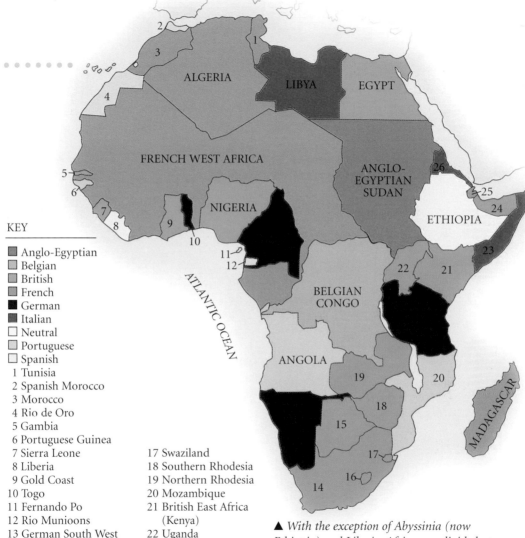

KEY
- Anglo-Egyptian
- Belgian
- British
- French
- German
- Italian
- Neutral
- Portuguese
- Spanish

1 Tunisia
2 Spanish Morocco
3 Morocco
4 Rio de Oro
5 Gambia
6 Portuguese Guinea
7 Sierra Leone
8 Liberia
9 Gold Coast
10 Togo
11 Fernando Po
12 Rio Munioons
13 German South West
   Africa
14 Union of South Africa
15 Bechuanaland
16 Basutoland
17 Swaziland
18 Southern Rhodesia
19 Northern Rhodesia
20 Mozambique
21 British East Africa
   (Kenya)
22 Uganda
23 Italian Somaliland
24 British Somaliland
25 French Somaliland
26 Eritrea

▲ With the exception of Abyssinia (now Ethiopia) and Liberia, Africa was divided up between various European countries. These colonies produced raw materials, such as metal ore, which were vital to the war industries.

63

The build-up to Loos

- **After the Second Battle of Ypres**, many British officers complained about the lack of artillery shells. It soon became clear that the Liberal government of Herbert Asquith had not ordered enough shells from the arms factories.

- **A furious row broke out** in the British Parliament, which newspapers called the 'Shells Scandal'.

- **Asquith was forced** to form a coalition government and appointed a new Minister for Munitions, David Lloyd George.

- **On 5 August 1915**, the Germans running occupied Belgium arrested a British nurse named Edith Cavell. She admitted helping British soldiers escape capture. The Germans accused her of being a spy.

- **Cavell** was put in prison. The Germans refused to allow either Belgian lawyers or diplomats from neutral countries to see her.

- **On October 11**, a German court found Cavell guilty of espionage. A British chaplain was allowed to see her for 30 minutes. The next morning she was shot by the Germans.

▶ *Nurse Edith Cavell, who was executed by the Germans for helping British soldiers to escape capture.*

- **Public opinion in many neutral countries** was outraged. People in the United States were particularly angry that the Germans had shot a female civilian nurse.

- **In July**, French commander Joffre promised the Russians that he would launch a major attack to divert German forces from the Eastern Front. He persuaded Britain's War Minister, Lord Kitchener, to order a British attack as well.

- **British commander in France**, Sir John French, still did not have enough artillery shells to prepare the way for a major attack. Kitchener told him to use poison gas instead.

- **When the Battle of Loos began**, the British heavy guns had only 90 shells each, the light guns just 150. French said, "We will achieve little other than to impress our allies with our sincerity."

▶ *The only defence against poison gas was to wear a mask, but these were heavy and restricted vision.*

65

The Battle of Loos

- **The Battle of Loos began** on 25 September, when poison gas was released by the British as a wind blew towards the German trenches. However, the wind changed direction and blew the gas back over the British lines.

- **When the British troops attacked**, the Germans were ready. The machine guns in the front line cut down thousands of men in the first few hours of the attack.

- **For the first time**, there were enough motor ambulances to evacuate the wounded back to hospitals once they had been carried off the battlefield by stretcher bearers.

- **Lieutenant Robert Graves**, later a writer, led his platoon to attack at Loos. When he reached the German trenches, only a single man was following. "Where are the men?" asked Graves. "Dead, sir," replied the soldier.

- **General Sir John French ordered his artillery** to fire every shell they had to help the infantry. On the second day, French called off the massed attacks, but continued with small-scale assaults until 8 October.

- **Of the 10,000 British soldiers who attacked** at Loos, 8200 were killed or wounded. The Germans called the battle 'The Graveyard'.

- **The French attack broke through** the German front line, but could not break the second line. Joffre claimed a great victory, but he had lost more men than the Germans.

◀ *The writer Rudyard Kipling never got over the news that his son had been killed at Loos.*

> **· · · FASCINATING FACT · · ·**
> On the afternoon of the first day, Lieutenant John Kipling was killed by
> a German shell. His father was the famous writer Rudyard Kipling,
> who never really recovered from the loss.

- **The British Parliament was furious** at the high casualties at Loos. Lord
  Kitchener was put in charge of recruitment. French was sacked.

- **The British appointed a new commander** in France, Scottish cavalry officer
  Douglas Haig. He had fought through the retreat from Mons and was liked
  and trusted. Haig had new ideas about how to fight the war.

▶ *German soldiers surrender to Indian
troops. Small-scale raids and local
attacks proved more successful than
the earlier massed assaults.*

Stalemate at Gallipoli

- **At Gallipoli the Australian and New Zealand Army Corps** (Anzac) had made little progress.

- **In May,** the man who had come up with the idea, Winston Churchill, lost his job as First Lord of the Admiralty. He took command of a battalion on the front line in France.

- **General Hamilton devised** a new plan. A British force would make a new landing at Suvla Bay to outflank the Turkish defences.

- **The Anzacs would attack** the hills of Sari Bair. The troops from Suvla Bay would then attack the Turks from the rear. Within 48 hours, Hamilton believed, Sari Bair would be captured.

- **Then the British and Anzacs could march** to the straits of the Dardanelles to secure the north shore. This would allow the British battleships to steam to Constantinople and open fire. Turkey would be forced to surrender.

▲ *A British Enfield .303 MkV rifle. With a magazine holding five bullets, the .303 was the standard British rifle of the war.*

- **On 6 August**, General Sir Frederick Stopford supervised the British landings in Suvla Bay, while the Anzacs attacked Sari Bair. They reached the crest of the hill and could see the Dardanelles, but could get no further.

- **Stopford refused to follow** the plan of attacking the Turks from behind. Instead he ordered his men to concentrate on landing supplies. When Stopford ordered an attack three days later, the Turkish commander had prepared his defences.

- **On 10 August**, Mustapha Kemal led a counter attack that pushed the Anzacs off the crest of Sari Bair.

- **Hamilton ordered Stopford** to attack again in September, but the offensive was a costly failure. In October Hamilton was sacked and never again held a senior command.

- **The naval officer Roger Keyes** who served at Gallipoli, drew up guidelines for future seaborne operations, which were later used in World War II, especially at Dunkirk and on D-Day.

▶ *An Australian war memorial commemorates the heroic spirit of the Australian troops at Gallipoli and the legendary 'mateship' shown towards each other by the fighting men.*

Bulgaria joins the war

- **The Kingdom of Bulgaria** had been formed in 1878 from the Ottoman provinces of Bulgaria and Rumelia, but did not become completely independent until 1908.

- **In the First Balkan War of 1911,** Bulgaria gained new territory from the defeated Ottoman Empire. The following year Bulgaria lost most of the new land to Serbia and Greece in the second Balkan War.

▶ *King Ferdinand of Bulgaria was famous for his wily diplomacy and cunning strategy.*

King Ferdinand was of German ancestry, but his people had links to Russia. Ferdinand managed to remain friendly with both empires, earning himself the name of 'Foxy Ferdinand'.

- **When World War I broke out**, Bulgaria remained neutral. However, King Ferdinand began expanding the Bulgarian army and equipping it with modern weapons. By the spring of 1915 he had 300,000 men ready for war.

- **King Ferdinand sent ambassadors** to both sides during the war. They emphasized that Bulgaria now had the largest army of all the Balkan countries and controlled the access of the river Danube to the sea.

- **The Bulgarian ambassadors also dropped hints** that Ferdinand was keen for Bulgaria to control the port of Alexandroupoli on the Aegean Sea and to regain the lands lost in the Second Balkan War.

- **The British were the first to respond** to Ferdinand. In return for Bulgaria declaring war on Turkey, they promised to give Bulgaria more lands from Turkey, and the port of Tekirdag on the Bosporus.

- **Ferdinand was impressed** by the British offer, but when the attack on Gallipoli failed, he believed that Britain could not deliver its promise.

- **Then Kaiser Wilhelm of Germany offered** Bulgaria as much of Serbia as it wanted, plus Alexandroupoli. As a sign of goodwill he sent the Bulgarian army dozens of modern German aircraft.

- **In August 1915**, King Ferdinand promised to declare war on Serbia whenever Germany asked. The Kaiser told Ferdinand to wait until a joint Austrian-German offensive on Serbia could be organized.

The defeat of Serbia

- **World War I began with a conflict** between Serbia and the Austrian Empire. However, there had been little fighting between them.

- **When German commander** in chief, Erich von Falkenhayn, learned that Kaiser Wilhelm had persuaded Bulgaria to join the Central Powers, he decided it was time to eliminate Serbia. Falkenhayn gave the task to General Mackensen.

- **On 5 October 1915,** the Germans crossed the Danube and within 48 hours had captured Belgrade.

- **Also on 5 October 1915,** the French–British force that had been heading for Gallipoli landed in the Greek port of Salonika. They began to march towards Serbia, but King Constantine, the Kaiser's brother-in-law, refused to help.

- **The Bulgarians declared war** on Serbia on 14 October. Their army crossed the border and headed for the key transport centre of Nis and the city of Skopje.

- **On 22 October,** the Allied advance from Salonika was stopped by the Bulgarians at Negotin. Nine days later the main Serb supply base of Kragujevac was captured by the Germans.

- **The Serbs retreated** southwest to Kosovo. Six hundred years earlier the Serbs had lost their independence when they lost a battle to the Turks at Kosovo.

- **On 23 November,** King Peter of Serbia ordered his men to destroy their artillery and wagons. He led them on foot into the Albanian mountains. He hoped to reach the Adriatic Sea to meet the British and French navies.

- **About a quarter of the Serb army** of 250,000 died in the snowy mountains.

- **In May 1916,** the Serb army was transported to Salonika. It was re-equipped with British weapons to prepare a march back into Serbia.

◀ *Serb machine gunners open fire as they protect the columns of the Serb army retreating into Albania.*

73

War in the air

- **When the war broke out**, all countries had a few aircraft that they intended to use for scouting purposes. The aircraft were made of wood, canvas and wire. They could fly at 130 km/h, but carried no weapons.

- **In November pilots began dropping** hand grenades or artillery shells on troops. Others carried shotguns and rifles with which to shoot aircraft.

- **By early 1915**, new types of two-man aircraft were being produced. The engine drove a propeller at the rear, while the gunner sat in the front with a machine gun. Some could carry a few light bombs.

- **Navigation was achieved** by looking at the ground and trying to spot a landmark. On most missions over half the pilots got lost.

- **The air crew** did not have any parachutes. Early parachutes were too big and heavy to fit in the aircraft.

- **One German pilot called** 'The Mad Major' by the British, would fly low over the trenches, then perform aerobatics before flying home.

- **On 1 April 1915**, the French pilot Roland Garros strapped a machine gun to the engine of his fast scout plane with a propeller at the front.

- **To stop the machine gun damaging** his own propeller, Garros fitted the blades with bullet-proof metal deflectors. By using the speed of his plane and aiming his machine gun at the enemy, he could outmanoeuvre any German aircraft.

- **In August**, the Germans countered with the Fokker EIII monoplane. The machine gun on this plane fired in time with the propeller, so that the bullets passed between the blades, removing the need for clumsy deflectors.

- **German pilot**, Oswald Boelcke, perfected new tactics to use with the new Fokker aircraft. By October the German squadrons ruled the air.

▲ *A German pilot uses the forward-firing machine gun on his Fokker Eindecker to shoot down a British gun bus. The Fokker was so deadly that British pilots called it 'the Fokker Scourge'.*

The Allies think again

- **On 6 December 1915,** the senior commanders of Britain and France met at the HQ of French Field Marshal Joffre to discuss how to win the war.

- **The failures of Gallipoli and Salonika** led the governments of France and Britain to believe that the war could only be won on the Western Front. Only if Germany were defeated, could the war end in 1916.

- **The new British commander** in France, Sir Douglas Haig, had to cooperate with Joffre, but he was not under Joffre and could make his own decisions.

- **The French called up vast reserves** of men and converted much of their industry to producing weapons. Joffre was confident that a new attack would break the German army.

- **Haig also had large reserves** of men and weapons available. However, he was unconvinced by Joffre's idea of yet another infantry attack.

- **A major recruitment drive** in Britain by Lord Kitchener, boosted by outrage over the German execution of Nurse Cavell, led to large numbers of volunteers.

- **Many of the volunteers joined up** as 'Pals' units. Groups of workmates or villages insisted on serving together.

▶ *The Welsh politician, Lloyd George, revolutionized the British armaments industry in 1915, ensuring that the army had enough weapons and ammunition to continue the war.*

▶ *This recruitment poster for the British army showed that the famous military hero Lord Kitchener was the most successful of the war and had become an iconic image.*

"YOUR COUNTRY NEEDS YOU"

- **Lloyd George had transformed** the munitions industry in the previous eight months. There were now more shells and guns than ever before.

- **Joffre suggested** a combined British–French attack on either side of the river Somme. Haig agreed, but he asked for time to consider the best way to make the attack.

- **Unknown to the Allies**, the Germans had their own plans – to move faster when the spring weather came in 1916.

The Kaiser's war plans

- **By the end of 1915**, Turkey and Bulgaria had joined the Central Powers – Germany and Austria. Germany was still faced by a war on two fronts.

- **The Austrians began to think** that they could not win. General von Höztendorf told his government on 4 January, "There is no question of destroying the Russian war machine."

- **German commander in chief**, Erich von Falkenhayn, and Kaiser Wilhelm decided to finish the war in the Balkans, by first crushing tiny Montenegro. The Austrians could concentrate on Russia.

- **A joint organized Austrian–Bulgarian** offensive smashed the Montenegran army in just nine days. On 17 January, Montenegro surrendered to Austria.

- **Falkenhayn studied** the Russian front. The German and Austrian armies were deep inside Russia, separated from their homeland by hundreds of kilometres of poor roads. Falkenhayn decided that a major offensive was impossible.

- **The Austrian army was ordered** to watch the Russians. After losing 2 million men in 1915, would the Russians be able to mount a major campaign?

- **To secure the Eastern Front**, the Kaiser promised the Poles, Latvians, Lithuanians, Estonians and others, independence after Russia's defeat.

- **These promises gave them a reason** to support Germany. He allowed the eastern states to set up civilian governments in areas occupied by Germany.

- **These changes allowed** the Germans to concentrate on the Western Front. The Kaiser had decided to beat France and Britain in 1916.

- **The Kaiser ordered** Falkenhayn to devise a plan to achieve victory. Falkenhayn decided to look at the history of France for an answer.

▲ *German infantry occupy a well-built front line trench to repel a British attack. Not all trenches were as well built or well maintained as this, though the German trenches were generally the best.*

Retreat from Gallipoli

- **Before the Allies could begin** to implement their plans for 1916, they had to draw to a close one of the failed operations of 1915 – Gallipoli.

- **In October 1915**, Sir Ian Hamilton was recalled to Britain. He was replaced by Sir Charles Monro. Monro spent a week studying the situation, then wrote back to London recommending instant withdrawal of all troops.

- **Lord Kitchener was sent out** by the British government to see the situation for himself. Kitchener thought that a fortified base should be built on Cape Helles and the other positions abandoned.

▼ *A British field gun is transported ashore in December 1915.*

> **. . . . FASCINATING FACT . . . .**
> On 27 November, a blizzard hit Gallipoli. Over 5000 men suffered
> frostbite and 300 died because of the cold.

- **The British government decided** to evacuate completely – the Cape Helles fortress was abandoned.

- **On 19 December**, the men at Suvla Bay and Anzac Cove were evacuated to waiting ships. The Australians invented a way of firing rifles automatically, so that it would appear that men were still present when they had in fact left.

- **On 8 January**, the final evacuation began at Cape Helles. All the men were evacuated without a single casualty. The Turks did not interfere.

- **In total, the Allies had seen** 252,000 men killed, wounded or captured at Gallipoli, out of 480,000 who took part. The Turks had lost 68,000 men killed and around 150,000 wounded.

- **The Allies also lost** a huge quantity of stores and ammunition, which the Turks gratefully gathered up. They then moved these supplies to be used against the Allies in other theatres of the war.

- **At the time**, many people thought the Gallipoli campaign had been a disaster. Later, military strategists thought that it had been a good idea that was badly implemented. Winston Churchill, who suggested the campaign, said, "We sent two-thirds of what was needed one month too late."

The Verdun Plan

- **Verdun on the river Meuse** had been fortified since the days of the Roman Empire. It was one of France's main army depots and a powerful fortress. In 1914 it had famously held out against a German attack.

- **German commander**, Erich von Falkenhayn, studied French history. He believed that the French would do almost anything to hold Verdun.

- **The area around Verdun** was a quiet sector. When a sudden flash flood washed away the earth between a German and a French trench, the men ignored their enemies while they dug new trenches.

- **The steep hills and deep gullies** of the area around Verdun were good for defence. On them the French had built a series of forts, each containing underground shelters and guns set in concrete and metal emplacements.

- **The most powerful** was Fort Douaumont. It had heavy artillery, light artillery, machine guns and kilometres of underground tunnels.

- **Falkenhayn decided to attack** Verdun, but with no intention of capturing the city or forts. He planned merely to pretend to try to capture them.

- **This would persuade the French** to pour reinforcements into Verdun. Once the French were within range, the German artillery would wipe them out.

- **Falkenhayn hoped to inflict** huge casualties on the French army, without the Germans losing many men. "We will bleed France white," he said.

- **Kaiser Wilhelm liked the plan** so much that he asked for Crown Prince Wilhelm, heir to the German throne, to be the commander. Falkenhayn arranged for experienced generals to have real control on the battlefield.

- **The French garrison at Verdun considered** that they were safe in their forts. They allowed the outer defences to fall into disrepair.

▼ *French troops man a reserve line trench at Verdun. The area has been churned up by intense artillery fire and stripped of vegetation.*

The Easter Uprising

- **Ireland had been ruled** by Britain for generations. In 1801, the Irish were given the right to elect MPs to the British Parliament in London. However, many Irish people wanted to govern themselves.

- **When World War I broke out**, thousands of Irishmen volunteered. A large proportion of the British army was made up of Irish regiments.

- **The British government was in the process** of granting Home Rule to Ireland when war broke out. It was postponed until peace was achieved.

- **In April 1916** a Sinn Fein leader, Roger Casement, was caught bringing German weapons to Ireland. He was hanged as a traitor in time of war.

- **Patrick Pearse drew up a plan** for around 1200 armed republicans to seize government buildings in Dublin. He hoped that the people of Ireland would then rise up against the British. Pearse thought the British would be too busy fighting Germany to suppress a mass rebellion.

- **On Easter Monday at 12 noon**, the Irish republicans struck. They seized five of their seven objectives with very little fighting. The British reacted by imposing martial law and blocking all roads in and out of Dublin.

- **On Wednesday**, British artillery began shelling the rebel strongholds. British commander, Sir John Maxwell, was ordered to put down the rising as fast as possible. He ordered infantry attacks to begin on the Thursday.

> **FASCINATING FACT**
> A few small groups supported using terrorism and warfare to drive out the British. They lacked manpower and weapons to make a real difference.

- **On Saturday**, the surviving rebels surrendered. Much of Dublin lay in ruins and around 700 civilians were killed, along with 500 rebels and 500 British.

- **Pearse and the rebel leaders** were executed a few weeks later. This act outraged many Irish who had opposed the Easter Uprising. In the election of 1918, Ireland elected a majority of MPs wanting independence from Britain.

▼ *Irish rebels defend ruined buildings in Dublin against British troops armed with machine guns.*

'They shall not pass'

- **By 21 February 1916**, the Germans had gathered 1200 artillery guns facing the French lines at Verdun. Of these, 500 were heavy guns. The guns had almost unlimited supplies of ammunition.

- **Just before dawn the German guns** opened fire. The French front line received the most intense bombardment of the war. At 4 p.m. the guns fell silent and German patrols went forward to test the defences. Enough French soldiers survived to drive them off. The guns began firing again.

▼ *A vast French cemetery at Verdun shows the sheer scale of the losses. Even more men were killed, but their bodies never discovered.*

- **For two days the Germans continued** making probing attacks. On 24 February the French broke. The Germans advanced rapidly.

- **Sergeant Kunze of the Brandenburg Regiment** reached Fort Douaumont at dawn on 25 February. He led his 45 men through an open door and found the French garrison eating breakfast. The most powerful fortress in the world had fallen.

- **Marshal Joffre sent** General Henri Pétain to take command at Verdun. Pétain announced, "They shall not pass."

- **Pétain built a new road**, the Voie Sacrée, to Verdun. Along this road, as planned by General Erich von Falkenhayn, French reinforcements arrived.

- **Meanwhile, French 75-mm guns** on the left bank of the river Meuse were firing into the German flank. German losses began to rise.

- **Crown Prince Wilhelm ordered** thousands of men to attack the French artillery. They captured some, but found more guns beyond them. Falkenhayn ordered a halt to the attacks.

- **In June the Germans struck again**, on a front line of just 5 km. Using poison gas, they breached the French lines and rifle bullets began hitting houses in Verdun town. Then, suddenly, the German attacks stopped. Only the artillery continued to fire.

The Brusilov Offensive

- **By early 1916,** Russian Tsar Nicholas II was permanently at army headquarters to act as commander in chief and boost his soldiers' morale. This left the Russian government in the hands of Tsarina Alexandra.

  - **The Tsarina was greatly influenced** by a debauched Siberian mystic called Grigori Rasputin. They promoted their friends instead of efficient and capable men. The Russian government began to decline in effectiveness.

  - **Tsar Nicholas ordered** Marshal Alexei Brusilov to attack the Austrians to distract attention from the main attack on the German army.

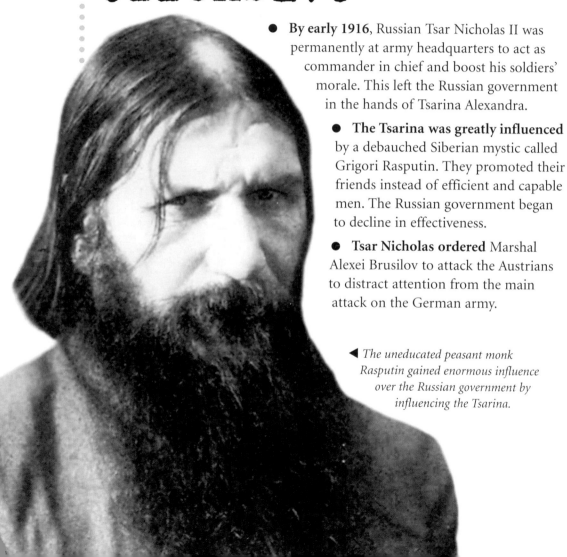

◄ *The uneducated peasant monk Rasputin gained enormous influence over the Russian government by influencing the Tsarina.*

The main Russian offensive started on 18 June, but halted almost at once when the men ran out of supplies and reserves were sent in the wrong direction.

- **Brusilov developed new tactics** for his attack. On 4 June, Brusilov's offensive smashed through the Austrian lines in three places. On 8 June, Austrian Archduke Josef Ferdinand had to abandon his birthday party when a Russian shell landed in the garden of the house where the party was being held.

- **For eight weeks**, the Russians advanced, but the attack came to a halt when General von Ludendorff moved German troops to support the Austrians.

- **Romania had remained neutral** when World War I began. King Ferdinand decided to see which side was going to win before committing his small kingdom. The Brusilov Offensive and optimistic reports from the Somme convinced him the Allies would win.

- **The Russians asked King Ferdinand** to attack Bulgaria. On 17 August, Romania declared war on Austria and invaded Transylvania, a Romanian-speaking province of the Austrian Empire.

- **Within six weeks the Romanian army** of 500,000 men had been crushed by a combined German–Austrian–Bulgarian offensive. The rich oil fields were in German hands.

- **Denmark, Norway and the Netherlands favoured** the Allied cause, but decided to remain neutral. They did not want to become another Romania.

Haig's new idea

- **In accordance with** the plans agreed in December, Sir Douglas Haig began preparing a major British offensive in the Somme area of northern France. He had 600,000 trained volunteers and a vast amount of artillery and shells.

- **Haig recognized** that conventional tactics had failed at Neuve-Chappelle and Loos in 1915. He and his staff questioned officers who had taken part in those battles and studied the problems of trench warfare in an effort to develop new, more successful tactics.

- **They decided** that the breaks in the German lines achieved in 1915 had been too narrow for reserves to push through – a wide front was needed.

- **Reserves had not moved** forwards fast enough to exploit the gaps in the German lines. This time the reserves would be sent forwards as soon as the first wave had reached the German trenches.

- **Gas was too unpredictable** for widespread use. Instead gas shells fired from artillery would be aimed at small targets, if the weather was suitable.

◀ *The British army of 1916 was made up of well-equipped volunteers. The uniform of a soldier consisted of a steel helmet to protect the head from shrapnel, lengths of cloth called puttees worn around the legs to protect from mud, waterproof boots and a tunic. Each soldier also carried a rifle and a bayonet. Bayonets were only used in close combat.*

- **Artillery fire** had missed many German defences. Aircraft would be sent up weeks before the attack to locate machine gun positions and bunkers so that they could be hit by artillery before the attack began.

- **A widespread breakthrough** was unlikely, so troops were given realistic objectives such as capturing particular hills or areas of German defences.

- **Cavalry would** be made ready just in case a breakthrough occurred. They were given explosive charges so they could demolish enemy railways and roads far behind the front line.

- **Previously the Germans** had guessed in advance where the attacks would take place. This time some areas that were not to be attacked would be shelled to confuse the Germans.

- **Unfortunately** for the British, the Germans had also been planning. They revised the weaknesses they saw at Loos and by the summer of 1916 had new types of defence.

▲ *A .38 calibre Colt double action revolver. A double action pistol required a stronger pull on the trigger to fire, so was less likely to go off by accident.*

First day on the Somme

- **British commander in France**, Sir Douglas Haig, planned his major attack in the Somme area for 15 August, when all his preparations would be made.

- **Marshal Joffre begged** him to attack earlier. Haig agreed to attack on 1 July. His junior officers were worried that the new plan would not be ready.

- **On 26 June**, a massive bombardment began. British guns pounded the German lines for five days, but many of the shells did not explode.

- **The British gunners did not realize** that the Germans had rebuilt many earth or sandbag defences in concrete. The light British shells did not damage them.

- **Most of the German soldiers** were safe in dugouts over 15 m deep beneath the Somme.

- **The bombardment ceased** at 7.30 a.m. on 1 July. The Germans raced from their dugouts to man the trenches and machine guns.

◄ *French troops race forwards across the smooth, grassy fields of the Somme area. French attacks in the south proved more successful than those of the British.*

- **The British began to advance** expecting most Germans to have been killed. The infantry advanced in four lines, about 100 m behind each other and with 4 m between each man.

- **The German machine guns mowed down** the first wave of British soldiers mercilessly. The Middlesex Regiment lost 622 men out of 740 in ten minutes.

- **The carnage was so horrific** that no messages got back from the first wave. According to plan, the second wave advanced and suffered similar losses.

- **By nightfall**, 20,000 British soldiers were dead and 40,000 wounded. Never before or since has the British army lost so many men in 24 hours.

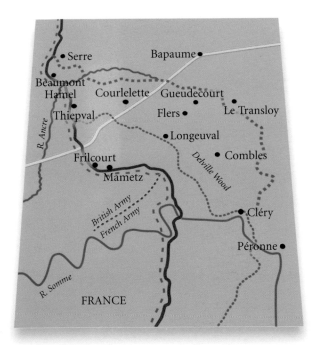

KEY

- - - Anglo-French front line: 1 July 1916

⋅⋅⋅ Anglo-French front line: 31 July 1916

▪▪▪ Anglo-French front line: 20 November 1916

⌐ German front line: 1 July 1916

═══ Bapaume road

◄ *The advances achieved on the Somme were much smaller than planned and casualties were higher than expected. The fighting ended without a decisive result.*

93

Death on the Somme

- **On 2 July**, British commander Sir Douglas Haig ordered the attack to continue. The reports he had received were contradictory and confused. He and his senior officers refused to believe that their plan could go so wrong.

- **By the end of 2 July**, Haig finally realized the true situation. The Ulster Division had taken the German front line. The 13 Corps captured the village of Montauban. Success was not achieved anywhere else.

- **Haig ordered for new attacks** to take place, to continue the advance of the Ulstermen and 13 Corps, and elsewhere for the useless attacks to cease.

- **On 14 July**, British General Henry Rawlinson suggested that his men should try the novel idea of attacking at night after a short, dense bombardment. Haig gave permission the next day.

- **The night attack took the Germans** by surprise. By dawn the British had broken through the German defences completely on a front line of 3 km. The infantry sent messages for the cavalry to advance.

- **A few cavalry units received** the messages and rode forward. They crossed the battered Somme battlefield, then emerged into open country and charged.

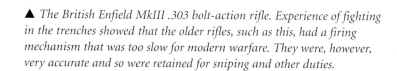

▲ *The British Enfield MkIII .303 bolt-action rifle. Experience of fighting in the trenches showed that the older rifles, such as this, had a firing mechanism that was too slow for modern warfare. They were, however, very accurate and so were retained for sniping and other duties.*

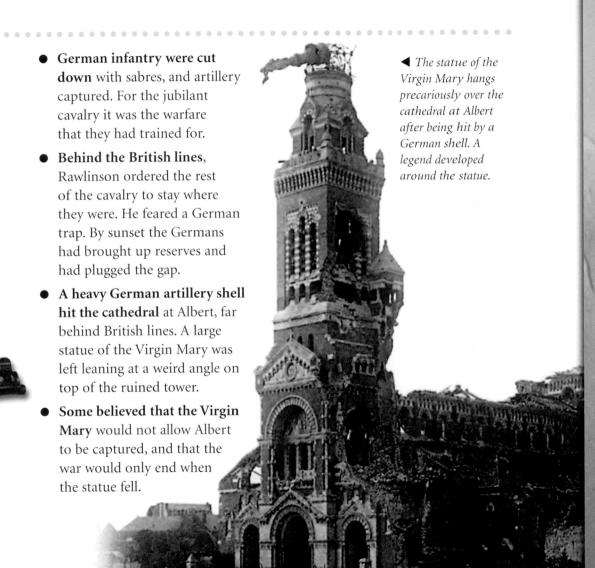

- **German infantry were cut down** with sabres, and artillery captured. For the jubilant cavalry it was the warfare that they had trained for.

- **Behind the British lines**, Rawlinson ordered the rest of the cavalry to stay where they were. He feared a German trap. By sunset the Germans had brought up reserves and had plugged the gap.

- **A heavy German artillery shell hit the cathedral** at Albert, far behind British lines. A large statue of the Virgin Mary was left leaning at a weird angle on top of the ruined tower.

- **Some believed that the Virgin Mary** would not allow Albert to be captured, and that the war would only end when the statue fell.

◄ *The statue of the Virgin Mary hangs precariously over the cathedral at Albert after being hit by a German shell. A legend developed around the statue.*

Enter the tanks

- **In August 1916**, General Rawlinson persuaded Sir Douglas Haig to try a new weapon that had been developed on the orders of Winston Churchill. It was called a 'land battleship', then the 'thingum-a-jig'. Finally it was named 'tank'.

- **The development of the tank** began in October 1914, when military engineer Colonel Swinton used tractors with caterpillar tracks to haul heavy equipment around the fields near Ypres.

- **It then occurred to Swinton** to build a larger tractor, then mount a gun on top of it. He could add a couple of machine guns as well.

▼ *A 'Big Willie' tank advances past a British rear trench. The large wheel at the rear was designed to help the poor steering mechanism, but failed in action and had to be replaced.*

- **In April 1915,** Swinton suggested encasing the guns and crew of the tractor in thick metal plates that would be able to stop all bullets and shrapnel. He drew up plans and sent the idea to the War Office.

- **Lord Kitchener dismissed** the idea, but Churchill was enthusiastic. He arranged for naval money to be spent developing the idea of the 'land battleship'.

- **Eventually there were two types** of tank. 'Big Willie' had two six pounder guns to destroy enemy strongpoints. 'Mother' was equipped with five machine guns.

- **When Haig ordered** Swinton to use his tanks on the Somme, Swinton was furious. He only had 50 machines, and was still having problems with the steering mechanism. Haig insisted.

- **On 15 September** the 28-tonne tanks lumbered forward at 5 km/h, impervious to all but heavy artillery.

- **By noon many had either run out of fuel,** broken down or been hit by artillery.

- **The excited tank crews were keen** to fight again, but wanted to devise special tactics. Swinton wanted to build new tanks of improved design.

▶ *Lord Kitchener was scornful of the idea of armoured fighting vehicles – tanks – but others were more enthusiastic.*

Air power's first strike

- **The Battle of the Somme** was the first time that aircraft played a significant part in the plans of senior commanders. British General Sir Douglas Haig ordered his airmen to scout behind German lines, and to shoot down any German aircraft that tried to scout behind British lines.

- **All sides were developing** specialist fighters, bombers and reconnaissance aircraft by 1916, but designs had remained fairly unaltered since 1915.

- **Reconnaissance aircraft began** to carry radios so that the observer could report back to base instantly.

- **It soon became clear** that reconnaissance planes and bombers could only operate if the fighters could keep the skies clear of enemy fighters.

- **The Germans relied** on the Fokker E series fighter, while the British produced increasingly effective 'pushers' such as the Vickers FB5 Gun Bus and the DeHavilland DH2.

- **During the Battle of the Somme** three new aircraft appeared. The British flew the Sopwith 1 $^1/_2$ Strutter, the French the Nieuport Scout, the Germans the Albatros D1. All were biplanes with synchronized guns pointing forwards.

- **German pilot Max Immelman invented** several aerobatic tricks useful in combat. The famous 'Immelman turn' allowed him to fire at an enemy, then flip over and back to fire again on the same target.

- **Another German**, Oswald Boelcke, developed tactics in which pilots could cooperate with each other in combat.

- **Boelcke insisted** that pilots flew and fought in flights of six, led by an experienced officer and all flying the same type of machine.
- **Several flights could be joined together** to form a 'flying circus'. These large formations were highly effective in controlling a given area of sky and shooting down any enemy that dared intrude.

▼ *A British two-seater scout aircraft drops a bomb on to German trenches. At first bombs were carried in the cockpit and dropped by hand, only later did proper bomb racks and aiming devices become the norm.*

Autumn slaughter at Verdun

- **The fighting at Verdun continued** throughout the summer of 1916.

- **On 11 July,** the Germans failed to take the remaining high ground in French hands overlooking Verdun. They did capture the heavily defended Fort Vaux, then ceased major attacks as they transferred men to the Somme.

- **As the intensity of fighting** at Verdun died down, General Pétain was replaced as French commander by the ambitious General Robert Nivelle.

- **Nivelle developed a plan** for retaking the ground lost to the Germans. A short artillery bombardment would be followed by infantry infiltration.

- **Infiltration involved** creeping forwards at night between German bunkers and strongpoints. These would then be attacked from all sides the next day.

- **It was hoped** that because the French soldiers would be mixed up with the German positions, the enemy would be unable to call in artillery fire.

◀ *A motor ambulance with the driver's seat protected by wet-weather covers. Wounded men evacuated quickly stood a much better chance of survival, so these vehicles were in high demand.*

- **Nivelle believed that infiltration tactics** would capture the individual strongpoints and hills around Verdun. He did not intend to break through.

- **Nivelle spent three months** building up his forces and using aircraft to map out the routes to be taken by his men.

- **On 24 October**, Nivelle's attack at Verdun began. The infiltration tactics were successful. Fort Vaux was captured in a few days and Fort Douaumont on 2 November.

- **By December** Nivelle's men had recaptured much of the lost ground, ending the Battle of Verdun. The Germans lost 230,000 wounded and 100,000 killed; the French lost 300,000 wounded and 162,000 killed.

▶ *A French unit rests in a trench. Note the poorly maintained sloping sides of the trench that indicate this is in a rear area.*

Silence over the Somme

- **After the tank attack** of September, the fighting on the Somme returned to small-scale attacks and retreats.

- **During the fighting**, British regiments began reporting 'trench fever', a disease spread by lice. It quickly spread to German and French units.

- **Trench fever began** with a splitting headache, then a high temperature and pains in the legs. It lasted five days, faded for a few days, then returned.

- **Soldiers who caught** 'trench fever' were unfit for duty for three weeks to four months.

- **By the autumn**, every man coming out of the line to rest had to strip, have a hot bath and have his clothes and kit fumigated. The disease faded that winter, but was never eradicated.

- **In early October** heavy rains lashed northern France. The chalk ground became slippery and waterlogged. Men found it difficult to move quickly.

- **On 18 November**, British commander Sir Douglas Haig ordered that all attacks should cease until the following spring. The British had advanced no more than 11 km. In many places they had failed to take the objectives set for the first day.

> ### FASCINATING FACT
> Haig was depressed by the failure and by the large casualties. He considered resigning, but King George V persuaded him to stay and promoted him to Field Marshal.

▲ *Injured British and German soldiers walk away from the Somme battlefield to British first aid posts behind the front lines.*

- **The British had lost** 95,000 dead and 320,000 wounded; the Germans lost 164,000 dead and 400,000 wounded; the French lost 50,000 dead and 140,000 wounded.

- **Haig now faced** a war of attrition – he would have to grind down the German army while protecting his men from unnecessary deaths. He was unable to carry out these aims.

103

Lawrence of Arabia

- **By the summer** of 1916, Turkey was doing well in the war. The Allies had been thrown out of Gallipoli in January and a second British army had been surrounded and captured at Kut in Iraq.

- **The British had defeated** a Turkish attack on the Suez Canal, but had been unable to advance far into Palestine. Then they gained an unexpected ally.

- **The Turkish Empire included** the vast Arabian peninsula. Most of the area was controlled loosely by the Turks, being ruled by Arab princes and tribal leaders who owed allegiance to the Sultan.

◄ *Dressed in Arab costume and fighting deep behind enemy lines, T E Lawrence became the most famous of several British officers working with the Arabs in the war against the Ottoman Empire.*

- **In June 1916**, the Hashemite princes of Hejaz rebelled against Turkish rule. The warriors of Sherif Hussein captured Mecca and Taif, but failed in an attack on Medina.

- **In October Britain sent** two officers from Egypt to try to reach Hussein and find out what was happening. Ronald Storrs and Thomas Lawrence reached Hussein and concluded that the Arab revolt would do little more than tie down a few thousand Turks.

- **Then Lawrence went on to meet** Hussein's younger brother, Amir Feisal. Feisal was a charismatic leader with several hundred Arab warriors under his control.

- **Lawrence persuaded** Feisal to abandon attacks on Medina in favour of raiding the railway line leading from Turkey to Medina.

- **The successes Feisal and Lawrence** had looting trains began to attract other Arab tribes to the uprising. By March 1917, Lawrence was dressing in Arab costume and accompanying the raiders on more daring missions.

- **In July 1917**, Lawrence persuaded Auda abu Tayi to lead the Howeitat tribe to attack the great Turkish port at Aqaba. By launching a surprise attack from the rear, the Arabs seized the port with ease.

...FASCINATING FACT...
Impressed by the capture of Aqaba, the British commander
Edmund Allenby, sent weapons, supplies and gold to Lawrence with
instructions to raise all the Arabs in revolt against the Turks.

War weariness

- **After the terrible losses** of 1915, and even more so after the summer of 1916, some people in most of the combatant nations became weary of the war.

- **However, the military commanders** of the major powers would not accept defeat. All armies remained intact and in high spirits.

- **Neither side was close to defeat**, though none was close to victory.

- **In Britain** the losses on the Somme led to a change of prime minister. Liberal Herbert Asquith was replaced by his fellow Liberal Lloyd George.

- **The British people were still determined** to gain victory over Germany. Despite the losses there were still plenty of recruits.

- **In France**, food prices were increasing and fuel was scarce. Trade Unions suggested that the war should be stopped given the hardships of the poor.

- **In December**, the French government responded by promoting Robert Nivelle to commander in chief with orders to win the war in 1917.

- **Russia was suffering** terrible economic problems. Food, fuel and clothes were all in short supply. In November, Tsar Nicholas asked the neutral Swedish government to suggest negotiations to the Germans. The Germans refused.

- **Emperor Franz Joseph** of Austria died in November 1916 and was replaced by Emperor Carl. The new Emperor was appalled by the state of the Empire's finances. He wanted peace, but dared not without German permission.

- **The president of the USA**, Woodrow Wilson, was willing to chair a conference to decide on a peace settlement. Both Germany and France set preconditions that the other would not accept. No conference was held.

▶ *A mobile soup wagon distributes hot food to civilians in the streets of Berlin. Fuel for cookers was in short supply, so wagons were the only way some people got hot food.*

Germany's peace note

- **On 12 December 1916** the world was staggered when German Chancellor Theobald Bethmann-Hollweg announced that Germany would make peace.

- **US President Woodrow Wilson** responded by suggesting that each combatant nation should draw up a list of what they were hoping to achieve if they won the war. He would then study the lists to see if a compromise was possible.

- **France replied with a list** of idealistic concepts, plus the solid demand that the area of Alsace-Lorraine should be given to France by Germany.

- **Britain wanted Belgium** to be recognized as an independent and neutral country, as it had been before 1914. It also wanted the German navy to be reduced in size, but it was clear there was room for negotiation on this point.

- **Italy stated** that it wanted to gain the Italian-speaking provinces of the Austrian Empire, and tried to claim some islands in the Adriatic.

- **Emperor Carl of Austria stuck** to the original demands made of Serbia in 1914, adding only that he would not make peace without Germany.

- **Tsar Nicholas of Russia** said that all he wanted was a return to the situation before the war, though he also wanted Serbia to be satisfied.

- **The rulers of Bulgaria**, Romania, Serbia, Montenegro and Turkey repeated their various war aims. They all accepted that the major powers would decide whether the war would continue or not.

- **The Germans then announced** that they would not negotiate through the USA. If any country wanted to make peace, they had to deal directly with Germany or not at all.

- **Britain and France** at once refused. The war went on.

▶ *The front page of the British newspaper, the* Daily Sketch, *reports the news of Germany's peace note. The photo montage shows the Kaiser holding a bloodstained sword and urges that the offer should be turned down.*

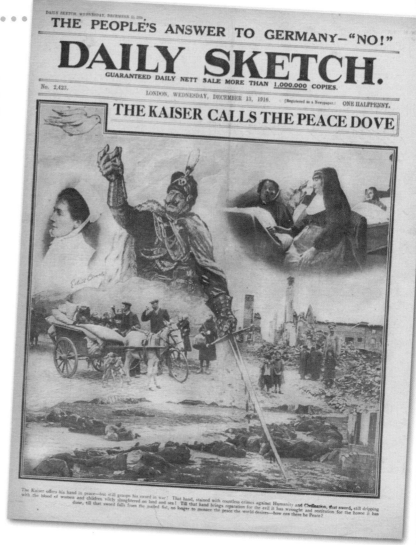

THE PEOPLE'S ANSWER TO GERMANY—"NO!"

DAILY SKETCH.

GUARANTEED DAILY NETT SALE MORE THAN 1,000,000 COPIES.

No. 2,425.   LONDON, WEDNESDAY, DECEMBER 13, 1916.   [Registered as a Newspaper.]   ONE HALFPENNY.

THE KAISER CALLS THE PEACE DOVE

The Kaiser offers his hand in peace—but still grasps his sword in war! That hand, stained with countless crimes against Humanity and Civilisation, that sword, still dripping with the blood of women and children vilely slaughtered on land and sea! Till that hand brings reparation for the evil it has wrought and restitution for the havoc it has done, till that sword falls from the mailed fist, no longer to menace the peace the world desires—how can there be Peace?

The role of sea power

◀ *The British victory at the Battle of Trafalgar in 1805 gave Britain control of the seas for over 100 years.*

- **Throughout history**, nations with coastlines have relied to a lesser or greater extent on sea power.

- **Island nations**, such as Britain, rely on sea trade when dealing with other countries. Those with some land frontiers are not so dependent.

- **In time of war**, sea trade becomes increasingly important. The economy of a nation can be seriously damaged if its sea trade is cut off.

- **Countries build warships** to attack each other's merchant ships and to protect their own. These warships are used to control the seas.

- **Although warships** are frequently used to fight each other, these battles are secondary to the main purpose of the war navies – to control sea trade.

- **In 1805**, the British Royal Navy totally defeated the French and Spanish fleets at the Battle of Trafalgar. Thereafter no country had seriously threatened its power.

- **Countries such as France**, the USA or Italy had fleets to protect merchant ships near their own coasts, but only Britain's could rule the world's oceans.

- **The British Empire included ports** and docks worldwide. The Royal Navy used these to service its ships so that they could operate almost anywhere.

- **Then one country decided** to try to challenge the might of the Royal Navy – Germany.

....FASCINATING FACT....
The key role of ships is economic. Ships transport goods
to and from other countries to be sold for profit.

The dreadnought race

- **The introduction of steam propulsion**, steel armour and long range, breech-loading guns revolutionized warship design and naval strategy.

- **By 1890**, most navies had decided that the future lay in battleships about 10,000 tonnes in weight and able to steam at 16 knots. Main armament would be four big 10- or 12-in guns.

- **Navies continued** to have specialist ships, but these were not expected to play a major role in sea warfare.

- **In 1896**, the Germans began to produce an entirely new form of warship – the cruiser. Smaller than battleships and armed with only medium guns, cruisers were able to steam at about 22 knots and could travel long distances without needing to resupply.

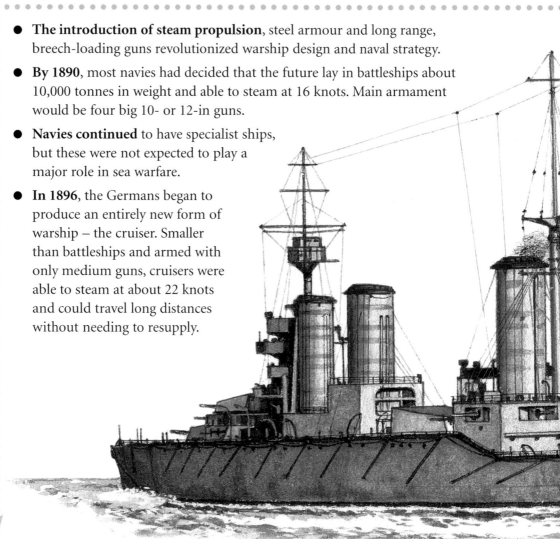

- **Cruisers could** disrupt sea trade far from their home ports, sinking merchant ships easily. If an enemy battleship approached they could escape at speed.

- **The German cruisers** were intended to threaten British merchant ships around the world. Britain began building its own cruisers to face the threat.

- **In 1906** the British began building HMS *Dreadnought*. This ship made all other battleships obsolete.

- *Dreadnought* **had ten 12-in guns**, thick armour and could reach 21 knots. She could outfight and outrun any other battleship in the world.

- **When Germany's Kaiser Wilhelm** saw *Dreadnought* he ordered Admiral von Tirpitz to build four similar ships for the German navy.

- **Britain responded with seven** more ships of the *Dreadnought* class. Rivalry between the British and German navies quickly gathered pace. Britain eventually built 48 dreadnoughts, and Germany 26.

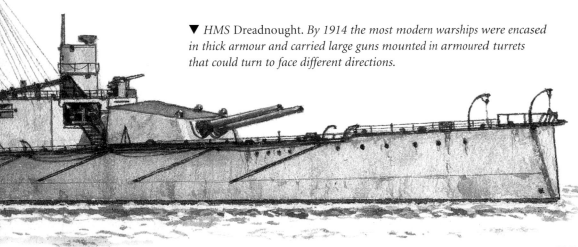

▼ HMS Dreadnought. *By 1914 the most modern warships were encased in thick armour and carried large guns mounted in armoured turrets that could turn to face different directions.*

113

Naval war begins

- **In the summer** of 1914, neither the British nor the German naval commanders expected to fight against each other. Even if war broke out, they thought it would be fought mainly on land and be over within weeks.

- **Nevertheless, both sides were prepared** for a major conflict. The Germans had a fleet based at Tsingtao in China made up of two heavy cruisers and three light cruisers.

- **In the Caribbean** the Germans had two light cruisers. In German East Africa was another modern cruiser, and two more were in the Mediterranean.

- **The main German force** was the High Seas Fleet, based in Germany. It consisted of 15 dreadnought battleships, 32 older battleships, four battle-cruisers, nine heavy cruisers, 14 light cruisers, 60 destroyers and various specialist ships.

▼ *The main British battle fleet was known as the Grand Fleet. It was the most powerful in the world in 1914.*

- **The Royal Navy was almost twice as large** as the German navy. However, the need to protect British merchant shipping meant that it was more scattered around the globe.

- **In the last week** of July 1914, Britain's First Lord of the Admiralty guessed that war was about to break out. He mobilized the Royal Navy for war and sent the Grand Fleet to take up battle stations in the North Sea.

- **The Grand Fleet successfully escorted** the troopships carrying the British Expeditionary Force to France. Then Churchill and his senior admiral, Prince Louis of Battenberg, planned offensive moves.

- **On 28 August**, two light cruisers and some destroyers were sent to attack German shipping in the Heligoland Bight. They were supported by the Battle Cruiser Squadron under Admiral David Beatty.

- **In the Heligoland Bight**, the two cruisers met six German cruisers and fled. Beatty then sank three German ships before he lost the rest in fog.

- **On 22 September**, a German U9 submarine, commanded by Lieutenant Otto Weddigen, sighted three British cruisers off the Hook of Holland. In less than 25 minutes the Germans sank all three British ships with torpedoes.

▶ *British Admiral David Beatty was one of the most successful admirals of the war. In 1919 he was made an Earl by King George V.*

The Battle of Coronel

- **On 23 August 1914**, Japan declared war on Germany. Friendly towards Britain, Japan wanted to occupy German-owned islands in the Pacific.

- **The Japanese fleet greatly outnumbered** the German Far East Fleet at Tsingtao. German Admiral Graf von Spee decided to take his ships to raid widely across the Pacific.

- **The German cruiser**, *Emden*, was sent to hunt merchant ships. With his other ships, Spee shelled French bases on Tahiti and cut the transpacific telegraph cable, then headed for Chile to attack merchant shipping.

- **On 1 November**, Spee met a British fleet commanded by Sir Christopher Craddock off Coronel. Spee had two heavy cruisers and three light cruisers.

- **Craddock had two heavy** and one light cruiser plus a converted merchant ship carrying light guns, but a British battleship lay just to the south.

- **At first Craddock sighted** only one German ship, so he moved to attack. By the time he realized his mistake, the fleets were within range of each other.

- **The German ships opened fire** at a range of 11,200 m. The British replied. It soon became obvious that the German ships were more stable in the rough seas, so their gunners could aim more accurately.

- **The two British heavy cruisers** were targeted by Spee and were quickly sunk. Admiral Craddock went down with his ship.

- **The British light cruiser**, *Glasgow*, and converted merchant ship *Otranto*, turned south, hoping to lure Spee towards the waiting battleship, *Canopus*.

- **Spee did not pursue** the British ships. The first fleet action between Britain and Germany had ended with a decisive German victory.

▼ *The German cruiser* Scharnhorst *at the Battle of Coronel, with* Gneisenau, *another ship, visible in the distance.*

The Battle of the Falklands

- **By late November 1914**, the ships of German Admiral von Spee were running short of fuel. He decided to leave the Pacific for the Atlantic. As well as hoping to sink merchant ships, Spee wanted to capture the Falkland Islands.

- **Port Stanley in the Falklands** was a major coal store for the Royal Navy, but was not heavily defended. Spee wanted to refuel and use the Falklands as a base from which to attack British shipping in the South Atlantic.

- **Unknown to Spee**, the British had reacted to their defeat at the Battle of Coronel by sending out a new fleet.

- **Led by Admiral Sir Doveton Sturdee**, the British fleet comprised two battle-cruisers and three cruisers. One of the cruisers was HMS *Glasgow*, which had narrowly avoided being sunk at Coronel.

- **Sturdee arrived at Port Stanley** on 7 December. His ships were taking on coal when the German fleet of Spee unexpectedly appeared over the horizon. It consisted of two heavy cruisers and three light cruisers.

- **The British battle-cruisers**, *Inflexible* and *Invincible*, each carried eight 12-in guns. The German heavy cruisers had only eight 8-in guns.

- **Realizing he was outgunned**, Spee steamed away at high speed to the southeast. Sturdee went to sea so quickly that he left crewmen on shore.

> ### FASCINATING FACT
> On 14 March 1915, *Dresden* was found by British cruisers off Juan Fernandez Island. Short of fuel and ammunition, the captain scuttled (deliberately sank) his ship.

- **The battle lasted** over eight hours. Both German heavy cruisers and two of the light cruisers were sunk as they raced across the South Atlantic.

- **Only the German** light cruiser *Dresden* escaped. The cruiser was to lead an adventurous career cruising and attacking across the South Pacific.

▼ *The British warship HMS* Inflexible *picks up survivors from* Gneisenau, *another ship, after the battle.*

Long range cruisers

▼ *German cruiser* Emden *is shot to pieces by Australian cruiser* Sydney. *The German ship was later beached on the island of Cocos.*

- **The first German cruiser to enter** the war was the *Goeben*, which shelled the French bases of Bône and Phillipeville less than 24 hours after war was declared. *Goeben* was accompanied by the light cruiser *Breslau*.

- **German cruisers** *Goeben* and *Breslau* arrived in Constantinople in October 1914. They officially became Turkish, but retained their German crews. They spent the war attacking Allied ships in the Mediterranean and Black Sea.

- **The cruiser *Königsberg*** was based in German East Africa. She sank British ships in the western Indian Ocean and shelled ports. She sank in July 1915.

- *Kronzprinz Wilhelm* **cruised** the Atlantic, sinking more than 20 merchant ships. In March she ran out of fuel and limped into Newport, where she was impounded by the USA.

- **The cruiser *Karlsruhe* sank** numerous merchant ships in the Caribbean. Her commander, Captain Kohler, moved to attack undefended Barbados, but his ship suddenly exploded and sank. None of the survivors could explain it.

- **The most successful cruiser** was *Emden*, nicknamed 'Swan of the East'. In August she left the German base of Tsingtao to raid Rangoon. Immediately the port was closed, disrupting British trade for over a month.

- **On 22 September**, *Emden* shelled Madras, setting fire to the vast oil stocks and destroying the docks.

- *Emden* **went** on to sink 23 merchant ships, a Russian cruiser and a French destroyer as well as blasting the docks of Penang to pieces.

- **On 9 November**, she met the Australian cruiser *Sydney* at the Cocos Islands. *Emden* ran ashore and was wrecked after a short battle.

- **After the war the cruiser** *Goeben*, renamed *Yawuz*, remained on active service with the Turkish navy until 1973.

England attacked

- **In 1914**, German and British fleets faced each other across the North Sea. The British were based at Scapa Flow in the Orkneys, the Germans at Kiel.

- **The British Grand Fleet** was made up of 28 dreadnought battleships, nine battle-cruisers, eight heavy cruisers, 26 light cruisers and 77 destroyers.

- **The German High Seas Fleet** had 16 dreadnought battleships, six battleships, five battle-cruisers, 11 light cruisers and 61 destroyers.

- **In general the German ships** were newer with more accurate guns and more effective armour than their British counterparts. However, the British commanders and captains tended to be more experienced.

- **Instead of one big battle**, the Germans intended to lure small sections of the British fleet to sea, then destroy them with a more powerful group of ships.

- **The campaign began** on 16 December 1914. A force of German battle-cruisers under Admiral Franz von Hipper steamed out of the mist to bombard Hartlepool and Scarborough. The ships shelled the docks and gun emplacements, but some shots hit the towns. Over 200 people were killed.

- **Six British destroyers** nearby came to investigate, but retreated when they realized the German ships were battle-cruisers. They radioed for help.

- **The British sent eight cruisers**, four battle-cruisers and six battleships to attack the Germans. Unknown to the British a much more powerful force of German battleships and cruisers lurked over the horizon.

- **However, the mist thickened** and a storm began. The two fleets missed each other in the bad weather and turned for their home ports.

- **The Germans believed** that their plan would have succeeded had it not been for the bad weather. They decided to try again when an opportunity arose.

▶ *A newspaper report details the damage caused by the German attack on Scarborough in December 1914.*

SCARBOROUGH SHELLED BY THE HUNS
THE DAMAGE DONE IN "THE QUEEN OF WATERING-PLACES"

WHERE 17 PEOPLE WERE KILLED AND 100 INJURED: A GENERAL VIEW OF SCARBOROUGH FROM SPA BRIDGE

HOUSE IN THE CRESCENT

HOUSE IN ST. NICHOLAS CLIFF

HOUSE IN LONSDALE ROAD

HOUSE IN COMMERCIAL STREET

SHELL DAMAGE TO THE TWELFTH-CENTURY CASTLE
Over 100 shells fell into the town. The pictures in the title show some of the fragments.

BIG GAPS BLOWN OUT OF CASTLE WALLS BY SHELL FIRE
The Town Hall, several churches and a number of other buildings were damaged.

The Battle of Dogger Bank

- **In January 1915** the Germans tried again to lure British ships to destruction. This time they did not attack British coastal towns, but British ships.

- **On 24 January**, German Admiral von Hipper led four battle-cruisers, four light cruisers and eight destroyers to attack the British fleet at Dogger Bank.

- **British Admiral David Beatty**, with five battle-cruisers, six cruisers and four destroyers, was protecting the fishing boats.

- **Beatty ordered his ships** to open fire. The German battlecruiser *Blücher* was badly damaged, as was the British flagship HMS *Lion*.

- **Major Harvey of the Royal Marines** won a Victoria Cross for leading the fight to save HMS *Lion*. He died of his wounds.

▼ *At the Battle of the Dogger Bank, the German cruiser* Blücher *was badly damaged, causing her to capsize. She later sank in the shallow waters with a great loss of life.*

- **Admiral Beatty signalled** his ships to chase the fleeing Germans while *Lion* attacked *Blücher*. The other captains misread the signal and attacked *Blücher* instead. The *Blücher* was sunk, but the other German ships escaped.

- **The Germans lost** 954 men killed, 189 taken prisoner and 70 wounded. The British lost 15 killed and 80 wounded. The British had won the battle.

- **A hit on the German battle-cruiser** *Seydlitz* started a fire that almost spread to the main ammunition store.

- **The Germans installed firewalls** around the ammunition stores on all their ships. This was to have a major impact at the Battle of Jutland (see page 136), when Hipper and Beatty met again in battle.

▲ *The Victoria Cross is the highest award for bravery given to British servicemen and women.*

> ...FASCINATING FACT...
> British battle-cruisers were known as 'The Big Cats' because some of them were named after wild cats.

Enter the U-boats

- **U-boats, or *Unterseebooten*, were German submarines** used to attack Allied merchant and naval ships. They came in various shapes and sizes, and were armed with guns, torpedoes or mines.

- **When the war broke out**, Germany had 33 U-boats in operation, with another 28 in construction. A few were 125-tonne ships able to operate only in coastal waters, but most were 200-tonne craft able to cruise the Atlantic.

- **U-boats were powered** to around 15 knots by diesel engines. As these needed air to work properly, they could only be used at the surface. U-boats used electric batteries when submerged. These lasted only a few hours and limited speed to 6 knots.

- **The rules of war allowed** enemy merchant ships to be sunk, but only after the crew had been given time to escape in boats. Neutral ships heading for an enemy port could be searched and any goods useful to the war effort could be destroyed or taken.

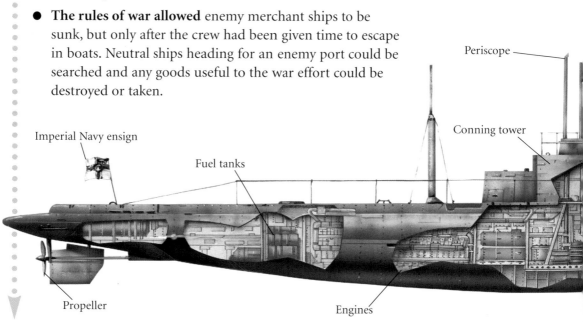

Periscope

Conning tower

Imperial Navy ensign

Fuel tanks

Propeller

Engines

- **Commanders found** the rules difficult to follow. Many merchant ships were faster than U-boats. It was more effective to sink enemy ships quickly.

- **On 4 February 1915**, Germany announced that it would sink all Allied merchant ships without warning in an area surrounding the British coast. Neutral ships were warned to make their nationality clear, or risk being sunk.

- **Kaiser Wilhelm II** was worried about possible civilian casualties. He insisted that U-boat captains should not sink passenger ships without warning.

- **Neutral nations**, especially the USA, protested fiercely to Germany. Some said they would declare war if their ships were sunk.

- **German Admiral von Pohl** ordered U-boat captains to sink ships without warning only if they were certain the target was Allied. If they were not certain they had to surface to find out, then open fire.

- **The period** that followed became known as 'restricted U-boat warfare'.

▼ *The German submarines, known as U-boats, proved to be one of the most effective new weapons to be used in World War I.*

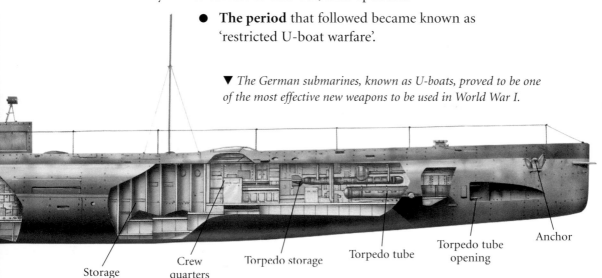

Storage

Crew quarters

Torpedo storage

Torpedo tube

Torpedo tube opening

Anchor

127

Q-ships

- **The restrictions placed** on commanders of U-boats meant that they preferred to surface when attacking a merchant ship. This allowed them to ensure the ship was an enemy, and to use their gun rather than torpedoes.

- **U-boats carried many shells** for the gun, but only a few torpedoes. Captains preferred to use their gun whenever possible.

- **Captains were supposed** to give the merchant crew time to get into boats before opening fire. Some merchant captains tried to radio for help, causing the U-boat captains to open fire at once.

- **In March 1915** the British began using Q-ships. These were merchant vessels with hidden guns. Q-ships were sent to waters known to be patrolled by U-boats.

- **If a U-boat surfaced** near a Q-ship, a few men would get into a boat and row away. When the U-boat approached, the hidden guns would be revealed. Q-ships had larger guns than U-boats and usually won the fight that followed.

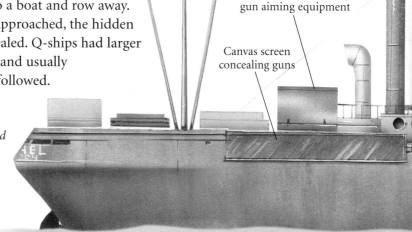

False cargo box hiding gun aiming equipment

Canvas screen concealing guns

▶ *The Q-ship appeared to be a harmless merchant ship, but sections of the ship's sides were made of canvas and could be taken down to reveal hidden guns.*

128

- **The most successful Q-ship captain** was Gordon Campbell. He was awarded a Victoria Cross, Britain's highest medal for gallantry.

- **It was illegal** for a merchant ship to fire on a warship. The Q-ships therefore carried naval crews and naval flags, but these were only revealed just before the Q-ship opened fire.

- **Q-ships were filled** with lightweight timber so that they were unlikely to sink if holed.

- **U-boat captains soon learned** about Q-ships. They began opening fire from a distance, and used torpedoes without warning on larger ships.

- **By late in 1916** the Q-ships were no longer effective. They were withdrawn from service.

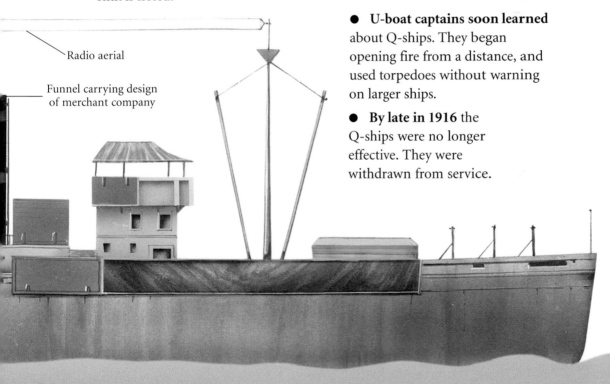

Radio aerial

Funnel carrying design of merchant company

Lusitania

- **By May 1915**, German U-boat commanders had become wary of Q-ships. Even unarmed merchant ships could cause problems by radioing for help from fast destroyers that patrolled waters near the British Isles.

- **It had become dangerous** for U-boats to surface and warn of an attack on merchant ships close to Britain. They tended to use torpedoes.

- **The German ambassador in the USA** issued warnings about U-boat activity. He told US citizens not to travel on ships passing close to Britain.

- **On 1 May 1915**, the unarmed British liner, *Lusitania*, left New York for Liverpool. It would be legal for a U-boat to sink her, but only if warning was given so that crew and passengers could escape.

- **At 2.15 p.m.** on 7 May the *Lusitania* was hit by two torpedoes fired by U20. Captain Schwieger gave no warning, having seen British destroyers nearby.

- ***Lusitania* was steaming** at high speed and developed a serious list (leaning to one side). It was almost impossible to launch the lifeboats and she sank.

- **American public opinion was outraged** by the attack. Former President Theodore Roosevelt said the sinking was 'piracy on a vast scale'.

- **US President Woodrow Wilson protested** to the Kaiser. The Kaiser publicly ordered that passenger liners must not be sunk without warning.

- **Secretly the Germans scaled back** their U-boat warfare. They did not want the USA to join the Allies.

> ### FASCINATING FACT
> Lusitania sank in only 19 minutes. In all, 1198 people died, of whom 128 were citizens of the USA.

A CRIME THAT HAS STAGGERED HUMANITY: THE TORPEDOING OF THE LUSITANIA

▲ The losses on Lusitania were particularly heavy because lifeboats could not be launched properly due to the way the ship tilted over as it sank.

The blockade of Germany

▼ *The British Grand Fleet at anchor in the Firth of Forth. The fleet was kept ready for instant action in case the German fleet was sighted at sea.*

- **When war began**, British First Lord of the Admiralty, Winston Churchill, ordered the Royal Navy to begin the blockade of Germany.

- **The English Channel was closed** to all ships, except those belonging to Britain or France on official war business.

- **The Shetland and Orkney islands** were patrolled by the Grand Fleet. They sank or captured any German or Austrian merchant ships they found.

- **Neutral ships were boarded** by British naval officers. If they were heading for Germany, they were searched. Goods likely to be useful to the German army or navy were seized. Such goods were called 'contraband'.

- **In March 1915**, the British navy established a search centre on the Orkneys. All merchant ships entering the North Sea were ordered to stop there, even if heading for a neutral country.

- **It was soon discovered** that the neutral countries were importing far more explosives, food, steel and other contraband goods than before the war.

- **The British began impounding** all contraband heading for neutral countries unless the ship's captain could prove it was not going to be passed onto Germany. The British government paid the market price for these goods.

- **In February 1916**, the British introduced a 'Black List of Companies' thought to be smuggling contraband to Germany. All their ships and goods entering the North Sea were confiscated without payment.

- **Many neutral countries**, including the USA, objected to the British blockade. The British refused to back down.

- **By the spring of 1916**, Germany was beginning to suffer shortages of key materials. The German navy was ordered to break the British blockade.

The High Seas Fleet goes to sea

- **Since the Battle of Dogger Bank**, Kaiser Wilhelm had refused to allow the large ships of the High Seas Fleet to go to sea. He wanted his navy intact to use as a threat during peace negotiations.

- **Sir John Jellicoe**, commander of the British Grand Fleet, also had orders not to risk his main force as this would leave Britain helpless against U-boats or invasion. It was widely said that 'Jellicoe is the only man on either side who could lose the war in an afternoon'.

- **The naval war was carried** on by U-boats attacking British merchant ships, and by destroyers and torpedo boats patrolling the North Sea close to the German coast.

- **Most of the North Sea** was in the complete control of the Royal Navy, which was therefore able to impose its blockade of Germany.

- **The Germans knew** that many neutral countries resented the British blockade, which was damaging their trade and cutting profits. However, the neutral countries would not take any real action so long as the British had unchallenged control of the seas.

- **In January 1916**, German Admiral Reinhard Scheer began sending his larger ships to sea on short patrols. These gave his men experience, but did nothing to convince neutral countries that he was able to challenge the Royal Navy.

- **The German moves** caused the British to move their battle-cruisers and their fast battleships from Scapa Flow to Rosyth.

- **The main British Grand Fleet** remained at Scapa Flow under the command of Jellicoe.

- **In April**, Scheer devised a plan to cripple the British Grand Fleet. He would send his U-boats to lurk unseen off Rosyth and Scapa Flow. Then he would take the High Seas Fleet to sea. When the British left port to attack, they would be sunk by the U-boats.

- **On 30 May 1916**, the German High Seas Fleet went to sea.

◀ *A flotilla of small British warships steams across the North Sea. The coal burned in the engines produced clouds of black smoke that could be seen from miles away.*

135

The Battle of Jutland begins

- **The initial plan** of German Admiral Scheer was abandoned because his U-boats were short of fuel. They were forced to return home before the weather cleared enough for the main fleet to go to sea.

- **Instead, Scheer planned** to send his battle-cruisers and cruisers, under Admiral Hipper, to threaten Allied merchant ships off Norway. This, he hoped, would lure the British battle-cruisers to sea where they could be sunk.

- **Radio signals ordering** the German battle-cruisers north were sent out for the British to intercept, while Scheer and his main battle fleet followed.

- **British Admiral Jellicoe learned** of the German signals and sent his battle-cruisers to sea under Admiral Beatty. However, Beatty also had the 5th Battle Squadron of four fast battleships, 12 cruisers and 28 destroyers.

- **Jellicoe then** took the Grand Fleet to patrol the sea to the north of Beatty.

▼ *HMS* Iron Duke, *the flagship of Admiral Jellicoe, fires its guns as it steams into action at the Battle of Jutland on 31 May 1916.*

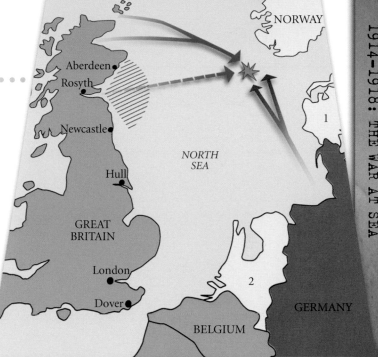

KEY

✶ Battle of Jutland

➤ Scheer's German battle fleet

➤ Jellicoe's British battle fleet

▪▪▪➤ Beatty's battle-cruiser fleet

▨ German submarines

1 Denmark
2 Netherlands

▶ *The Battle of Jutland was fought in the North Sea. Neither the British nor German commanders realized that they faced the main battle fleet of their enemy.*

- **Beatty steamed** towards Norway, with cruisers and destroyers spread out in front to scout for the Germans.

- **Meanwhile, Hipper was heading** north with five battle-cruisers behind a screen of four cruisers and 33 destroyers.

- **At 2.15 p.m.** the British cruiser *Galatea* saw smoke to the east and set off to investigate. It proved to be from a Norwegian merchant ship. The German cruiser *Elbing* was also investigating. At 2.30 p.m. the cruisers opened fire.

- **The two cruisers radioed** to their admirals that they were in action. Beatty and Hipper ordered their ships to head towards the battling cruisers. At 3.48 p.m. the rival battle-cruisers opened fire on each other.

- **The Battle of Jutland** had begun, almost by accident.

137

The Battle of Jutland ends

- **Around 4 p.m.** British battle-cruiser *Indefatigable* and *Queen Mary* suddenly blew up. The explosions were triggered by fires in the ammunition stores.

- **When British Admiral Beatty's** four battleships came in sight, German Admiral Hipper fled south.

- **Hipper's move was a trick** designed to lure Beatty towards the High Seas Fleet of German Admiral Scheer. At 4.33 p.m. Beatty was astonished to see the entire High Seas Fleet come over the horizon.

- **Beatty turned his ships** around, exchanging fire with the leading German ships. His ships were heavily outgunned, but he hoped to lure the Germans towards British Admiral Jellicoe who was now steaming south at full speed.

- **At 6.15 p.m.** the two mighty battle fleets sighted each other. The leading ships on both sides opened fire, pounding the enemy with heavy shells.

- **Unknown to the British**, many of their shells were faulty – they exploded on impact on the German armour rather than penetrating before exploding.

- **Scheer ordered his destroyers** to launch a mass of torpedoes at the British battleships. While Jellicoe manoeuvred to evade them, Scheer fled.

- **Further manoeuvring** meant that at sunset Jellicoe was between Scheer and Germany. Jellicoe hoped to begin the battle again at dawn.

- **British destroyers sighted** a damaged German battleship, *Pommern*, and mistook it for the main German fleet. Jellicoe turned in the wrong direction. By dawn on 31 May, Scheer was steaming rapidly for home.

- **John Cornwell won a VC** at Jutland, aged just 16. He stayed at his gun on HMS *Chester* even though the crew had been killed. He died of his wounds.

▲ *The letter home written by John Cornwell before he won his VC. The 16-year-old boy died in Grimsby hospital of his wounds three days after the battle.*

The U-boats return

▲ *Torpedoes being loaded into a German U-boat from a supply ship. By restocking their stores, fuel and weapons, U-boats could remain at sea for long periods of time.*

● **When the Battle of Jutland was over**, both sides studied the results. The British had lost three battle-cruisers, three heavy cruisers and eight destroyers; the Germans one old battleship, one battle-cruiser, four light cruisers and five destroyers.

- **The British had lost more ships**, and more important ships. Scheer realized that he had been lucky to escape with his fleet intact.

- **It was decided** that the German fleet would not go to sea again, but be retained as a threat in peace talks. The war would be continued by U-boats.

- **German supreme naval commander**, Admiral von Tirpitz, had resigned due to ill health in March 1916. He was replaced by Scheer, who also retained command of the High Seas Fleet.

- **On 24 March 1916**, a cross-channel ferry named *Sussex* was sunk without warning by a U-boat. Two US citizens were injured. Furious messages were exchanged between the American and German governments.

- **The dispute between the USA** and Germany ended in August when Germany promised to abide by the rules of war. President Wilson warned that if Germany broke its promises then the USA would join the Allies.

- **In January 1917**, the new commander of the German Army, Paul von Hindenburg, told the Kaiser that the army could not mount a war-winning offensive in that year.

- **German Chancellor Bethmann-Hollweg suggested** that Germany should concentrate on U-boat warfare.

- **In January 1917**, U-boats had been sinking an average of 320,000 tonnes of Allied shipping each month. If all restrictions on U-boat captains were lifted, it was thought the total would rise to 600,000 tonnes each month. Neutrals would probably cease trading with Britain.

- **German Chancellor Bethmann-Hollweg** thought Britain would make peace within six months. Kaiser Wilhelm agreed and the U-boats were unleashed.

British convoys

- **In January 1917**, Germany announced that it would commence 'unrestricted U-boat warfare' on 1 February. The USA immediately cut off all diplomatic relations.

- **The new style of U-boat warfare** meant that in a large area around the British Isles, the Germans could sink any ship without warning.

- **The Germans justified** this by stating that all ships bringing goods to Britain were helping to fight. It did not matter if the ship itself were neutral, nor what goods it carried. The Germans claimed it was a legitimate target.

- **In only the first month** of unrestricted U-boat warfare, sinkings almost trebled in number.

- **Within weeks it became clear** that the British would be starving by September if something were not done to stop merchant ships being sunk.

- **On 19 June**, British Admiral Jellicoe told the government that he could not guarantee food supplies unless the U-boat bases in occupied Belgium were captured.

- **The British government ordered** General Haig to launch an offensive to capture the ports. After months of bloody fighting, the attack failed.

- **In April**, seven US merchant ships were sunk after the USA declared war on Germany. US President Wilson reacted by refusing to send large numbers of troops to France unless their safety at sea could be guaranteed.

- **On 24 May**, the Royal Navy introduced convoys in the Atlantic.

- **On specified dates**, up to 50 merchant ships leaving a port in Canada or the USA would be escorted by one cruiser, six destroyers, 11 armed fishing boats and two fast motor gunboats.

▼ *A British naval airship flies above a convoy of merchant ships. From above, the crew of the airship could spot U-boats lurking beneath the surface of the sea and warn the convoy to alter course away from danger.*

Starvation looms

- **In June and July 1917**, only merchant ships not in convoy were lost to U-boat attack.

- **In June, a flotilla of American destroyers** arrived in Britain. The first convoy they escorted was attacked by U-boats, but no ships were lost.

- **The convoy system doubled** the numbers of U-boats being sunk by the Royal Navy each month to four. However, the Germans were building U-boats faster than they were being sunk – they were winning the war at sea.

- **As convoys reduced** the effectiveness of torpedoes and guns against merchant ships, the Germans made increased use of mines. Vast numbers were laid in and around British ports.

- **In August 1917**, a German motor gunboat sank the British merchant ship *Brussels* in the North Sea and captured her crew. The commander of the *Brussels* was Captain Charles Fryatt, who on an earlier voyage had fought off a surfaced U-boat by ramming it with his ship.

- **The Germans put Captain Fryatt** on trial for taking part in the war. After a one-day trial held behind locked doors, Fryatt was shot.

- **Neutral countries turned** against Germany. They were appalled that U-boats were allowed to sink without warning and that merchant ships were not allowed to fight back.

> ### FASCINATING FACT
> A U-boat crew heard a Morse Code message: 'Surface or I will explode my depth charge'. It surfaced and was captured, but there was no depth charge. A diver had done it to see what would happen.

▼ *Naval mines were dropped from ships or submarines. When they reached the sea floor, the metal arms opened out to serve as anchors, while the mines rose on steel cables to predetermined positions.*

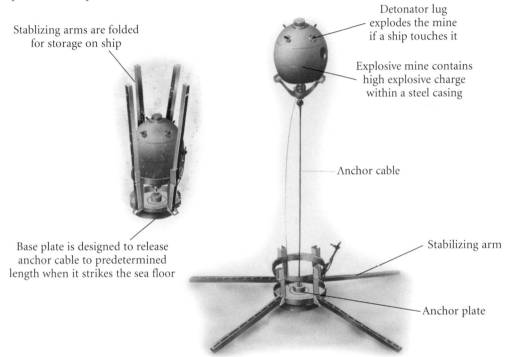

Stablizing arms are folded for storage on ship

Detonator lug explodes the mine if a ship touches it

Explosive mine contains high explosive charge within a steel casing

Anchor cable

Base plate is designed to release anchor cable to predetermined length when it strikes the sea floor

Stabilizing arm

Anchor plate

- **In October 1917** the British perfected an underwater mine. They laid hundreds in the Straits of Dover, blocking the main route to the Atlantic.

- **On 6 December** a French ship, *Mont Blanc*, loaded with ammunition, was part of a convoy assembling in Halifax, Canada. It suddenly exploded, killing 1600 people and wounding 9000 more.

War at sea ends

- **By January 1918** it was clear that the U-boats were failing to starve Britain into surrender. However, they continued to inflict great losses on the merchant ships.

- **German surface warships** remained a problem. Two cruisers attacked a convoy near Norway, sinking nine merchant ships and two British destroyers. The Royal Navy was now desperate for a knockout blow.

▲ *The entrance to the harbour at Zeebrugge is blocked by old ships deliberately sunk by the British. The port was out of action for weeks.*

- **A plan was devised** by British Admiral Sir Roger Keyes to block Zeebrugge, which was extensively used by U-boats.

- **Keyes' plan involved** sinking three old cruisers filled with concrete in the harbour mouth, while two submarines packed with explosives would moor alongside the harbour wall, then be blown up. The German defences would be distracted by the landing of marines.

- **The naval raid on Zeebrugge** successfully blocked the harbour to all but the smallest craft. It was weeks before the Germans had the port working again.

- **In April 1918**, the British learned that the powerful German High Seas Fleet was once again at sea, steaming north along the Norwegian coast. The Germans just missed two large convoys, which they could have destroyed.

- **Before the British Grand Fleet** could reach the area, the German fleet had returned to Germany.

- **On 18 October**, German Admiral Scheer ordered all U-boats to return to port. On its way back, one U-boat sank the *Saint Barcham* merchant ship in the Irish Sea. It was to be the last ship torpedoed in the war.

- **On 27 October**, Scheer issued orders for the High Seas Fleet to steam up the Thames and attack London. There was an immediate mutiny. The sailors refused. The war at sea was over.

· · · FASCINATING FACT · · ·

In February 1918, a liner carrying 2400 US troops was torpedoed and sunk in the Atlantic. All but 210 men were rescued.

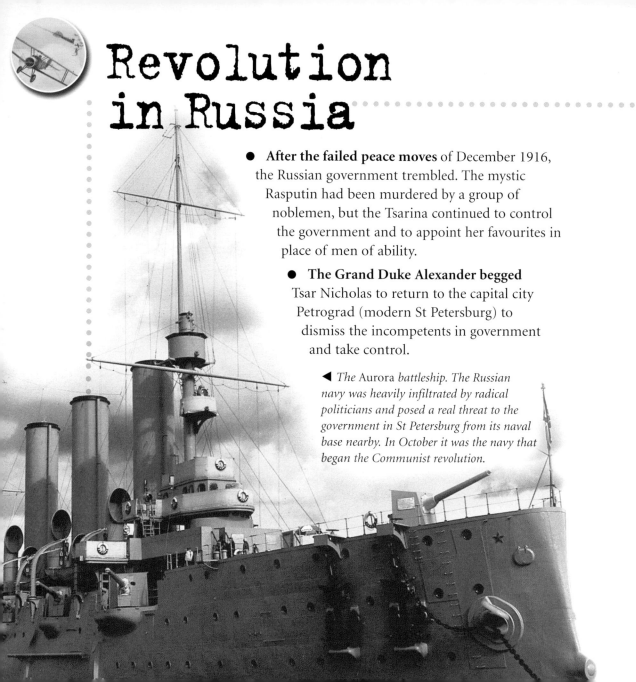

Revolution in Russia

- **After the failed peace moves** of December 1916, the Russian government trembled. The mystic Rasputin had been murdered by a group of noblemen, but the Tsarina continued to control the government and to appoint her favourites in place of men of ability.

  - **The Grand Duke Alexander begged** Tsar Nicholas to return to the capital city Petrograd (modern St Petersburg) to dismiss the incompetents in government and take control.

◀ *The Aurora battleship. The Russian navy was heavily infiltrated by radical politicians and posed a real threat to the government in St Petersburg from its naval base nearby. In October it was the navy that began the Communist revolution.*

- **The Chairman of the Duma**, or Council of State, Rodzyanko, wrote to the Tsar warning that if nothing was done to ease the conditions of workers in the industrial cities, there would be serious trouble.

- **Tsar Nicholas refused** to leave the command of his armies. However he sent General Khabalov with a force of 100,000 soldiers to impose martial law on the capital city.

- **On 7 March**, the workers in a few factories went on strike. Many went to the large Nevsky Prospect open square in St Petersburg, carrying banners demanding more food at cheaper prices. The next day more factories went on strike.

- **On Sunday 11 March**, vast crowds, of up to half a million, seethed through St Petersburg. Demonstrations took place in many cities at the same time.

- **When Khabalov ordered** his army to take to the streets, most refused. Some men shot their officers and went over to the side of the demonstrators. Even the most loyal Cossacks refused to leave barracks, being too frightened of the vast crowds.

- **On 15 March**, Tsar Nicholas finally visited St Petersburg. His train was surrounded by crowds of workers before it reached the city. Nicholas abdicated the throne in favour of his popular brother Michael. However, Michael refused.

- **For the first time in its history**, Russia did not have a monarch. A provisional government had to be elected and was then instructed to draw up a new constitution.

- **The first decision** of the provisional government, led by Alexander Kerensky, was to continue the war.

America declares war

- **When war broke out in 1914,** the USA remained neutral and was not directly affected by divisive European issues.

- **Many USA citizens in 1914** were immigrants from Europe. They tended to support their mother countries in the war.

- **The USA quarrelled** with Britain in the autumn of 1914 when the Royal Navy began stopping US ships from steaming to Germany.

- **It was agreed that no goods** likely to be useful to the war effort would be sent from America to Germany, but that peaceful trade could continue.

- **In February 1915,** a serious quarrel broke out with Germany. The German navy said that without notice it would sink any ships heading to Britain.

- **President Wilson told Germany** that he would declare war if any US ships were sunk. When *Lusitania* was sunk and many Americans killed, he moved to break diplomatic relations. Germany called off the campaign.

- **American public opinion** was outraged by the execution of Edith Cavell. Stories of German behaviour in occupied areas also upset Americans.

- **On 31 January 1917,** Germany once again announced unrestricted warfare on merchant ships. Wilson again said he would declare war if any US ships were sunk.

- **On 1 March,** German plans to persuade Mexico to attack the USA were discovered. American public opinion turned firmly against Germany.

- **On 20 March** a U-boat sank an unarmed American merchant ship. On 6 April 1917, the USA declared war on Germany.

▶ *In front of the US Congress, President Wilson asks for a vote to declare war on Germany. The vote was carried by an overwhelming majority.*

- **Just two months after the USA declared war** on Germany, General John Pershing arrived in France to take command of the American Expeditionary Forces in Europe. In fact it was an empty gesture as there were no such forces.

- **The USA had a population of 93 million**, larger than any belligerent country except Russia, and produced 45 million tonnes of steel each year, more than any country in the world.

◀ *An American recruitment poster of 1917 shows 'Uncle Sam', a popular cartoon figure that represented the Federal government of the USA.*

- **However, the vast wealth**, manpower and industrial output of the USA was being used for entirely peaceful purposes. It would take time to turn the USA into a great military power.

- **When the USA entered** the war, the US army consisted of 190,000 men spread in small detachments across the country and in the few overseas possessions. They were mainly used for police or peacekeeping duties and had no experience of modern warfare.

- **The armed forces lacked** the necessary equipment. There were few tents, no field hospitals and virtually no cold weather clothing. American soldiers tended to stay in base during bad weather.

- **The Americans had no heavy artillery**, nor many machine guns. The British offered to lend the Americans the guns they needed, but Pershing preferred to wait for his own weapons.

- **They also had no experience** of moving armies across any land except their own, and almost no idea how to feed and supply a large force in the field.

- **It would clearly be months** before the Americans would make much difference on the battlefields of Europe.

- **By 31 October 1917** there were 86,000 US troops in France. They were put into a quiet sector of the front line to gain experience of real combat.

The Nivelle Offensive

- **In February 1917,** the new French commander, General Robert Nivelle, tore up the plans agreed by his predecessor with the British. He had a bold, new plan.

- **"We have the formula for victory,"** declared Nivelle. He wanted to use the infiltration tactics so successful at Verdun, but on a massive scale.

- **Nivelle planned to attack** on a 50-km front around Soisson and Rheims with 5000 guns and one million men. He said he would break through in three days.

- **Nivelle's confidence** and charismatic personality boosted French morale. But by explaining his plan to the troops, Nivelle gave away the element of surprise.

- **The British attacked** Arras on 9 April, a week before the French offensive, to divert German reserves. Canadian troops captured Vimy Ridge.

- **Nivelle's offensive began** before dawn on 16 April with a short, well-aimed bombardment of German positions. However, the Germans had resited most of their guns as they had expected the French bombardment.

- **When the French infantry advanced**, they found much of the barbed wire intact. This slowed them down so that they could not infiltrate.

- **Since the French last scouted** the area of the attack, most of the German strongpoints had been moved and new ones built.

- **The repositioned German machine guns** began firing. Casualties were high.

- **After two weeks**, the French had captured the German front line, but not reached the second line. Around 225,000 Frenchmen were killed or wounded.

▶ *British lancers ride through Arras in April 1917 on their way to the front line. Cavalry were prepared in case a breakthrough was achieved, but they were never used.*

154

French mutiny

▼ *British soldiers cross a wrecked canal on a narrow wooden bridge. The British army was entirely unaware of the French mutinies until weeks later.*

- **On 29 April**, a French infantry regiment paraded prior to returning to the front line. When ordered to march, the men refused. They said they would not take part in another suicidal attack ordered by General Nivelle.

- **On 4 May**, another infantry regiment refused to move. On 16 May, three more refused to obey orders to attack.

- **The disorder swept through** the French army like wildfire on 28 May. Soon, men of 54 divisions were disobeying orders. Nivelle had only two loyal divisions. He put them in the front line to defend the trenches.

- **A regiment at Soissons hijacked** a train to Paris on 30 May, determined to invade Parliament. Officials diverted it.

- **On 1 June**, a regiment at Tardenois assaulted their officers, then rioted through the town for two days.

- **At Esternay thousands of soldiers invaded** the railway station demanding trains to take them home. More rioting followed.

- **The French government concealed** what was happening. Not even British commander Sir Douglas Haig knew about the mutinies. The Germans did not attack.

- **As the mutinies and rioting** reached a peak in the first week of June, Nivelle was sacked and General Pétain became the new commander in chief.

- **Pétain listened to grievances** and promised changes to pay and conditions. He arrested men who had used violence, but peaceful demonstrations were not punished. By 20 June the mutinies had ceased.

- **The French Parliament chose** a new prime minister, George Clemenceau. Together Clemenceau and Pétain worked to restore French morale and fighting ability.

New British tactics

- **Over the winter of 1916–17**, the British under General Sir Douglas Haig had once again been devising new tactics and plans. General Sir William Robertson told King George V, "It is no longer a question of aiming at breaking through the German lines. It is now a question of attacking limited objectives with the minimum loss."

- **The British studied** French General Nivelle's infiltration tactics and decided that they would be useful for small attacks to capture specific features.

- **The tactic of attacking at night**, used the previous year on the Somme, was a success. The staff officers decided to use it on a larger scale in future.

- **Infantry officers reported** that they had most success when they attacked as soon as the artillery barrage stopped. Artillery officers suggested improving on this with what they called a 'creeping barrage'.

- **A creeping barrage meant that the artillery** aimed slightly further away with each shot fired. Infantry could therefore move forwards just behind the last exploding shell without fear of being hit.

- **Engineers suggested** tunnelling underneath the German trenches and planting large quantities of explosives. These mines could blow up a German strongpoint from underneath, as effectively as an artillery shell could be falling on top of it.

- **Infantry found** that the German artillery knew where British front line trenches were. If the Germans suspected an attack, they would pound those trenches.

- **Instead of gathering** in the main trenches for an attack, the infantry were ordered to crawl on hands and knees into shell holes or dips in the ground. The German artillery missed them when it hit the trenches.

- **The Royal Flying Corps** (RFC) promised to bomb German supply dumps and transport links immediately behind the lines with accuracy. This would hinder the German defence.

- **The new tactics were tried out** on a small scale at Arras in April, prior to the main French attack under General Nivelle. They proved very successful and all the limited objectives were captured in just 48 hours.

▶ *A British howitzer fires on the German lines. Howitzers were guns that fired heavy shells over a short distance. They were useful in battles where the front lines did not move quickly.*

Trench raiding

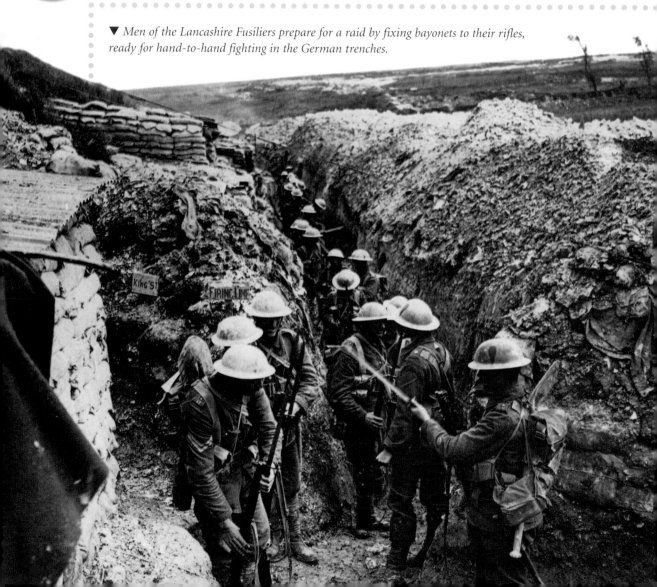

▼ *Men of the Lancashire Fusiliers prepare for a raid by fixing bayonets to their rifles, ready for hand-to-hand fighting in the German trenches.*

- **One of the most important new tactics** devised by the British was the 'trench raid'.

- **Ever since late 1914**, patrols had launched small night attacks on enemy front trenches. These early raids were designed to kill a few Germans and find out their unit, for intelligence purposes.

- **Throughout 1915 and 1916**, regiments made larger raids. Up to 100 men would cross to the enemy trenches. After a short fight, they would return.

- **British commander Sir Douglas Haig** now ordered that all regiments should mount a large raid once a month and smaller raids whenever possible.

- **Small raids continued** to involve only a dozen or so men. They tried to creep into enemy trenches, kill a few sentries and return without being seen.

- **These raids were intended** to worry the Germans on the front line, make them nervous and stop them from relaxing at any time.

- **Larger raids might involve** up to 500 men. They were carefully planned in advance and had specific objectives, such as planting explosives to demolish a strongpoint or to demolish a section of German trench.

- **Some officers formed** special raiding units that were highly skilled at these attacks. Other officers did not approve of raiding as it could cause casualties without achieving any real gains.

- **All raids gave the British** experience of warfare and were useful for getting new recruits accustomed to fighting and the trenches.

- **Throughout the summer** of 1917 raids took place all along the British section of the front line and continued until the end of the war.

Messines Ridge

- **After the success** of the limited offensive at Arras in April, British commander Sir Douglas Haig decided to try the new tactics again in May.

- **General Sir Herbert Plumer** suggested that the objective of the attack should be the capture of Messines Ridge. It dominated the area around Ypres, allowing the Germans on top of the ridge to direct artillery.

- **His plan involved** engineers tunnelling 19 huge mines underneath the German trenches, packed with 500 tonnes of high explosive.

- **Plumer planned** that after the mines were blown, his infantry would move forwards behind a creeping barrage, supported by tanks. He hoped to take the ridge with minimal losses to his own men.

- **Before the attack**, Plumer insisted that no men or guns should move during daylight. They had to remain hidden under camouflage nets and move only at night. The Germans had no idea that an attack was about to take place.

▼ *British troops move towards the front line in June 1917. Units nearing the battle zone were ordered to move in loose lines so that they did not form a dense target for German artillery.*

- **At 3.10 a.m.** on 7 June, the mines exploded. The German front line was completely wiped out. British, Australian and New Zealand troops waiting to advance were knocked off their feet. The blast was heard as far away as Bedford, England.

- **The creeping barrage** began immediately, while the tanks lumbered forwards and the infantry began to advance.

- **By noon**, the British had captured most of Messines Ridge and were digging new trenches to defend their gains.

- **German counter attacks continued** for five days. The British held firm. Victory was complete.

Third Battle of Ypres

- **On 19 June**, British Admiral Jellicoe told the government that U-boats operating from Belgium were sinking so many British merchant ships that, unless something were done, the country would soon run out of food.

- **The government ordered** their commander in France, Sir Douglas Haig, to capture the Belgian ports from the Germans.

- **General Hubert Gough was in charge** of planning the attack. He decided to use the new tactics, but with a heavy artillery bombardment.

- **On 31 July**, the attack began after the artillery had pounded the German positions for almost two weeks.

- **At Polygon Wood**, the Scottish Black Watch regiment was led into battle by a piper in full dress uniform playing the regimental march on his bagpipes.

- **That evening it rained**, and it continued for almost a week. The heavy artillery bombardment had destroyed the drainage system of the Flanders Plain, which turned to mud.

- **On 16 August**, Gough told Haig that because of the mud, he would be unable to capture the ports. Haig ordered Gough to continue with smaller attacks.

- **September passed** without much rain, so the plain dried out. Haig put General Plumer in charge of a new attack to capture Passchendaele Ridge.

- **Plumer planned and carried out** four advances that captured most of the ridge by early November. Then heavy rains began again. The land turned to liquid mud in which survival was difficult and fighting impossible.

- **After the battle ended** it became clear that the Royal Navy was sinking more U-boats than ever before. The food supply to Britain was safe after all.

▼ *The fighting at the third Battle of Ypres, commonly known as Passchendaele, was hampered by heavy rains and the clay soil that formed thick, sticky mud.*

Knights of the air

- **By early 1917**, air warfare saw aircraft specializing in the three roles of scouting, bombing and fighting other aircraft.

- **The Germans and French publicized** their successful pilots in newspapers, books and films. The French called them 'aces', and the word spread.

- **Albert Ball was a British pilot** who shot down over 40 German aircraft and invented new tactics. He was shot down and killed in May 1917.

- **British James McCudden shot down** 54 enemy aircraft, but was killed when his engine cut out when taking off.

- **Captain G H McElroy was a British ace** and he shot down 42 Germans. He vanished on a routine patrol and no one knows what happened to him.

- **American Raoul Lufbery led a group** of Americans who volunteered for the French air force before America joined the war. The squadron was known as the Escadrille Lafayette. He was shot down when attacking a German scout in May 1917.

- **The most successful ace** was German Baron Manfred von Richthofen. Between November 1916 and his death on 21 April 1918, he shot down 80 British and French aircraft.

> **FASCINATING FACT**
> Canadian Billy Bishop shot down 72 German aircraft. The Canadian government did not publicize individual achievements during the war.

▲ *A British pilot in his Sopwith fighter watches a burning German Albatros pass by. At this date most pilots did not have parachutes, so combats were often fatal.*

● **Richthofen was widely known** as the 'Red Baron' because he painted his aircraft completely red. All aircraft in his squadron had red patches. His brother, Lothar, was also an ace pilot who shot down over 40 aircraft.

● **After Richthofen's death** his squadron was taken over by another ace – Hermann Goering. He later joined the Nazi Party and led the German air force in World War II.

The Battle of the Zeppelins

▲ *By flying at high altitude the Zeppelins managed to evade British defences for many months. They dropped bombs on British cities, bringing terror and destruction in their wake.*

- **Before the war** German Count Ferdinand von Zeppelin developed a type of huge airship for long-distance passenger flights. As soon as the war broke out, the airships were taken over by the German army.

- **Zeppelin's airships had a metal frame** containing large bags of hydrogen gas, which lifted the craft into the air. They were powered by engines mounted outside the craft. Crew and bombs were carried in a gondola slung underneath.

- **The Zeppelins entered combat** on 26 August 1914, when one bombed Brussels. For the next six months, Zeppelins bombed army units in France and patrolled over the North Sea.

- **On the night** of 19 January, two Zeppelins bombed the docks at King's Lynn and Great Yarmouth, England. Four people were killed. Other raids followed and much damage was inflicted.

- **Between January and June 1915**, the RFC made 79 flights to attack Zeppelins over England. No Zeppelins were shot down, but eight aircraft crashed and three pilots were killed when trying to land in the dark.

- **On 6 June**, RFC pilot Reginald Warneford managed to get above a Zeppelin returning from a raid. He dropped six bombs, one of which hit the airship and exploded. The Zeppelin crashed in flames.

- **Most Zeppelins flew too high** for British aircraft to catch and attack them. There were never more than 20 Zeppelins in operation, but they bombed Britain almost at will.

- **By the summer of 1917** new British fighters were in operation. The Sopwith Camel was able to fly as high as the Zeppelins. Armed with incendiary bullets, Sopwith pilots could shoot them down.

- **Zeppelins continued** to patrol the North Sea and mount occasional raids, but by Christmas 1917, the Zeppelin menace had been beaten.

- **From October 1917**, Germany started to send large multi-engined bomber aircraft to attack London and towns in southern England. These Gotha and Staaken aircraft inflicted some damage, but British defences were able to limit the number that got through.

The Battle
of Caporetto

- **By the summer of 1917** the war in Italy had dragged on for two years. The Italian and Austrian armies had faced each other in the valley of the river Isonzo and in the Alps.

- **The Italians were never strong enough** to inflict serious losses on the Austrians, who had put most of their efforts into defeating the Russians. The battles fought on the river Isonzo were short and bloody, but inconclusive.

- **In September** the Italian commander, General Luigi Cadorna, ordered an end to all attacks as his forces were short of artillery shells.

- **Around the towns of Caporetto and Tolmino** there was little fighting, as the roads were used for a major offensive.

- **During August and September**, Italian-speaking Austrians fraternized with the Italians. They talked about how their families were suffering at home. It was a trick to undermine Italian morale in the quiet sector.

- **At 2 a.m. on 24 October** a massive bombardment was unleashed on the Italians around Caporetto. Vast numbers of German infantry attacked.

- **Overwhelmed**, most Italians fled, but some surrendered. By 10 a.m. the Germans had broken through the Italian lines, opening up a 24-km gap.

- **On 26 October**, Cadorna ordered his entire army to retreat. If they had stayed in the Isonzo Valley, they would have been surrounded.

- **Cadorna tried to organize** a defence on the river Tagliamento, but the Germans broke through again. The Italians retreated to the river Piave.

- **The Germans and Austrians** could not keep up with the swift Italian retreat. The Italians were able to escape and organize a defence that held.

◀ *The Italian army retreats from the Isonzo front in 1917. The Italians had fought well, but were overwhelmed by the sudden attack at Caporetto.*

Lenin's revolution

- **After the fall of Tsar Nicholas II**, the Russian Duma (parliament) elected a republican government led by the Socialist leader Alexander Kerensky.

- **Kerensky decided** that Russia would honour all agreements made by the Tsar, expecting other countries to honour their agreements with Russia.

- **As a result**, Kerensky kept Russia in the war. He promised that no offensives would be ordered and trusted that Germany would not attack Russia.

- **In September**, Kerensky had army commander General Kornilov arrested for alleged mutiny against the republic, deeply demoralizing the army.

- **Meanwhile, led by Vladimir Lenin**, an impoverished nobleman who had turned against the Tsarist regime, the Communists plotted a new revolution.

- **Communist activists joined** the committees, known as soviets, that had been elected by factory workers, peasant farmers, soldiers and others to voice their demands to the Kerensky government.

- **In September**, the collapse of the food distribution system brought hunger to the cities and to the army. Strikes broke out, organized by the Communists who blamed Kerensky.

◄ *Russian soldiers carry red cloths on their bayonets as they drive through the streets to show that they have joined the Communist forces.*

- **On 6 November**, Lenin ordered the Red Guards to seize the key public buildings in the capital, St Petersburg.

- **A shot fired** by the battleship *Aurora* signalled the final assault. Red Guards stormed the Winter Palace to arrest the provisional government.

- **Lenin agreed peace** with Germany. Russia handed over vast areas of land in return, allowing Lenin to enforce Communist rule on Russia. Now Germany could turn to the west to gain outright victory.

▼ *Communist revolutionary leader Vladimir Lenin toured the soviets of St Petersburg making a series of powerful speeches to stir up anger against the government. Behind him stands Leo Trotsky, who organized the Communist armed forces.*

173

The Arabs triumph

▼ *British soldiers march into the city of Kut on 3 March 1917. The rapid advance up the Mesopotamian valley secured local oil supplies for the Allies.*

- **In July 1917** an Arab force working with British liaison officer T E Lawrence captured the port of Aqaba from the Turks. This prompted many Arabs to join the uprising against Turkish rule.

- **British General Allenby was commanding** a British–Indian force in Palestine. He asked Lawrence to persuade the Arabs to coordinate their campaign with his own.

- **In October 1917**, Lawrence led the Arab armies of Sherif Hussein of Mecca to cut the Turkish supply railways near Amman in Syria.

- **On 6 November**, Allenby attacked the Turks at Beersheba. After ten days of fighting, his men reached Jaffa. The Turks fell back into Syria.

- **On 9 December**, Allenby and his army marched into Jerusalem. He became the first Christian soldier to enter the holy city since the Crusades over 700 years earlier.

- **Lawrence and Hussein's younger brother**, Amir Feisal, led the Arabs on numerous raids and attacks across the desert areas behind the Turkish lines.

- **Lawrence wore Arab clothes**, rode camels and lived among his Arab fighters.

- **Sherif Hussein established** complete control around the Muslim holy cities of Mecca and Medina. The Allies promised him that after the war was over, the Arabs would be free of Turkish rule. Hussein thought this meant they would be under his rule.

- **A British–Indian army reached Kut**, where a British army had surrendered to the Turks in 1916. Then it moved on to cut off Persia from Turkey.

- **By the spring of 1918**, Arabs who were loyal to Hussein and led by Lawrence were rampaging through the areas of the Turkish Empire inhabited by Arabs.

Marching from Salonika

- **For two years since the defeats** at Gallipoli and the crushing of Serbia, an Allied army had been camped around the Greek city of Salonika.

- **The army largely consisted** of the surviving Serb army, plus British, French and Australian troops evacuated from Gallipoli. Plans to attack Bulgaria or Austria had come to nothing due to lack of supplies and transport.

- **Greek King Constantine was married** to Sophie, sister of Kaiser Wilhelm of Germany. He did not wish to antagonize his brother-in-law, so he refused the Allies permission to move out of Salonika.

- **The Allies preferred** to keep Greece friendly, so they tried to persuade King Constantine to change his mind. By the summer of 1917, Greek public opinion had turned against Austria.

- **In June King Constantine abdicated** in favour of his son Alexander who appointed the anti-German, Eleutherios Venizelos as prime minister. On 2 July 1917, Greece declared war on Austria, Bulgaria, Turkey and Germany.

- **In December 1917**, the commander at Salonika was replaced by French General Franchet D'Esperery. D'Esperery had travelled extensively through the Balkans before the war and knew the area well. He was known as 'Desperate Frankie'.

- **He told his officers**, "I expect from you savage energy," and demanded a plan to attack northwards within 19 days.

- **Not until July** did D'Esperery have enough lorries and carts to transport his army and supplies over the Balkan mountains to face the armies of Austria and Bulgaria.

- **In August the forces at Salonika** were given permission by the British and French high commands to move north. Stores and supplies began pouring into Salonika onboard British ships.

- **On 15 September**, D'Esperery led his men north, heading for Bulgaria.

▼ *The Allied army marching north from Salonika was a mixed force made up of men from several different nations who spoke more than five different languages and had no agreed method of fighting.*

The Treaty of Brest-Litovsk

- **In November 1917** the Russian Communists, led by Lenin, established control over the vast Russian Empire by carrying out a daring coup in the capital, St Petersburg.

- **In December 1917**, Lenin agreed a ceasefire with Germany, and sent his deputy Leon Trotsky to Brest-Litovsk in Poland to negotiate a treaty with Germany and Austria. Trotsky was told to get peace at almost any price.

- **The Germans were keen** to annex large sections of the Russian Empire, or to see them set up as German-dominated independent nations.

- **The Austrian Empire** was on the point of economic collapse.

- **Once in Brest-Litovsk**, Trotsky came to believe that Germany and Austria were ripe for a Communist revolution, and if he could delay a peace treaty revolutions would break out.

- **In February 1918**, the Germans told him that unless he signed a treaty immediately, the war would begin again. Trotsky refused. The Germans invaded Russia.

- **The Russian forces** did nothing to halt the German advance.

- **By 24 February**, the German armies were approaching St Petersburg in the north and were on the river Don in the south.

- **On 3 March**, the Russians signed the Treaty of Brest-Litovsk. Poland, Latvia and Lithuania were annexed from Russia to Germany. Ukraine was set up as an independent country, but was occupied by German forces.

- **Former Tsar Nicholas II** was shot by the Communists in July 1918.

▶ *A photograph of the former Tsar Nicholas II with his family taken while they were prisoners of the Communists.*

Germany turns west

- **Two days after the Treaty of Brest-Litovsk** was signed, Germany, Bulgaria and Austria signed a peace treaty with Romania. The Treaty of Buftea forced Romania to hand the province of Dobrudja to Bulgaria, but gave Bessarabia, which had belonged to Russia, to Romania.

- **As soon as the treaties** of Brest-Litovsk and Buftea were signed, the Germans began their preparations for a mighty offensive in the west. Hundreds of railway trains steamed east to carry German armies from Russia to France.

▼ *Field Marshal Paul von Hindenburg (with walking stick) and General Erich von Ludendorff (facing camera on left) meet with German officers in Brussels.*

Ludendorff believed that if Germany had not beaten Britain and France by the autumn of 1918, it would lose the war.

- **The German army was now in the hands** of two men – General Paul von Hindenburg and General Erich von Ludendorff.

- **Hindenburg was the more senior**, but Ludendorff was the logistics genius. He alone knew how to move and supply the large armies of Germany.

- **In July 1917**, Ludendorff had calculated the relative strengths in manpower, supplies and money of the various countries involved in the war.

- **Ludendorff estimated** that by spring 1919 neither France, Germany nor Austria would be able to continue fighting. Britain, he thought, would be able to continue only at sea, while Turkey would be exhausted but would not be under serious attack.

- **Only the USA**, Ludendorff thought, would be stronger in 1919 than in 1917. By then, America would have mobilized an army of over 2 million men and would be using its great wealth to manufacture huge supplies of weapons.

- **American forces would prove** to be decisive in 1919. They would win the war and impose a peace on Europe drawn up in America.

- **Ludendorff believed** that the British might continue the war alone if France were defeated, but that France would not fight on if Britain were knocked out. Ludendorff decided he had to defeat the British. He then drew up his plans accordingly.

The Ludendorff Offensive

- **German General von Ludendorff** had drawn up plans over the winter of 1917 for defeating the British. Each meant massing the men and guns brought from Russia in a solid attacking block. In the end he chose two.

- **'St Michael' would be launched** first as an attack near St Quentin designed to split the British from the French. If that did not work, 'St George' would drive through Armentiéres and push the British into the sea.

- **Ludendorff and his staff** had devised new tactics. Each unit was divided into three waves. They had grenades, flame throwers and light machine guns.

- **These 'stormtroopers' were to race** past strongpoints and jump over trenches to reach the rear of the British lines. They would stop any reinforcements reaching the front line.

- **The second wave**, equipped with rifles and grenades, would capture the trenches. The third wave would tackle emplacements and bunkers.

- **The next day**, the Germans would repeat the manoeuvre until they had broken through. The cavalry and infantry would complete the victory.

- **At 5 a.m.** on 21 March 1918 the Germans unleashed a barrage by 6000 guns on a front of 64 km. It was the heaviest and best-aimed of the entire war.

▲ *The German Luger automatic pistol had bullets stored in the grip, allowing this model to fire more bullets before reloading than the revolvers used by the British.*

- **At 9.40 a.m.** the bombardment at the British rear areas and the German infantry swarmed forwards.

- **In the south**, the Germans did even better than planned. By evening the Germans were right through the British trenches.

- **Further north**, the British held onto the rear defences, though they had lost their forward positions. On 24 March the British retreat began.

▼ *Elite German infantry practise the new stormtrooper tactics behind the lines in the weeks before the attack.*

Ludendorff's failure

- **As the Germans surged forwards**, the senior British, French and American commanders met at Doullens. They agreed that they needed a supreme commander to coordinate the response to the German attack.

- **On 26 March**, they chose French General Philippe Pétain. He took the title General in Chief of the Allied armies in France.

- **Meanwhile, the RFC flew** hundreds of bombing attacks, but they began to run out of bombs.

- **At Hamel, an American brigade** went into battle. They had not yet had time to train in the use of their machine guns. One man had to read from the instruction booklet, while others were shooting at the Germans.

▶ *A heavy howitzer with its barrel aimed to hurl shells at a high trajectory. Shells falling steeply on to enemy defences penetrated deep into the soil before exploding. This allowed them to burst under concrete defences and shatter them.*

▶ *Equipped with a small gun and carrying only three men this light tank could move quickly to attack enemy infantry, but was highly vulnerable to artillery fire.*

- **On 24 March**, the Germans had built seven monstrous 15-in guns with a length of over 40 m. The shells could reach Paris.

- **The guns were positioned** around the town of Laon and fired shells at regular intervals. They killed many civilians and spread alarm through Paris.

- **On 29 March** the German attack began to lose power. There were enormous difficulties transporting supplies forwards over the shattered landscape.

- **Several German units** took to looting. One entire regiment became drunk after capturing a chateau stocked with thousands of bottles of wine.

- **On 9 April**, the Germans began their St George offensives. British commander Sir Douglas Haig issued a famous order, "With our backs to the wall and believing in the justice of our cause, each one of us must fight on to the end."

- **By 24 April** the new attack had been defeated.

America in action

- **After the mighty German attacks** had been halted by the British, the Allies believed that General Erich von Ludendorff had used up all his troops and ammunition brought from Russia. They were wrong.

- **The Blücher Offensive was aimed** at the French sector under the command of General Duchesne. The area had long been a quiet sector. Duchesne did not believe in the new tactics, nor had his men maintained their trenches.

- **Part of the line was held** by British troops from the Somme, who had been brought here to rest. Their officers asked for timber and sandbags to improve the trenches, but Duchesne refused to hand over valuable equipment.

- **On 27 May** the Germans struck. After a whirlwind bombardment, the stormtroopers poured forwards, supported by their second and third waves.

- **Duchesne refused** to believe that the Germans could break his lines, so he failed to order key bridges over the river Aisne to be blown. The Germans poured across the river Aisne and by nightfall were at the river Vesle.

- **As the Germans poured** towards Paris, French General Pétain asked US General Pershing to send his men in to hold the line.

▲ *A Smith and Wesson Model 1917 .45 calibre revolver. The heavy bullet fired by this gun was able to knock a man backwards with ease.*

- **The first complete American division** to enter battle was the 3rd Division which marched into Château Thierry in the afternoon of 31 May. The men spent three days digging in, before the Germans arrived on 3 June.

- **The next day** the US 2nd Division entered battle at the town of Lucyle-Bocage. As before, the German advance ended due to lack of supplies and poor discipline.

- **Ludendorff had lost** almost 25 percent of the men he had had in February. Some units began to argue about orders they did not like.

- **The Germans** began moving relatively unfit and poorly trained men up to the front. Ludendorff and Hindenburg were becoming worried.

▼ *American infantry struggle to reload their heavy machine gun during a training operation in France. To begin with, US soldiers suffered from inadequate training in modern warfare.*

The Habsburg Empire trembles

- **In 1914 the Habsburg Empire** was a complex and multi-national state united only by the fact that the whole area was ruled by the same monarch.

- **During the war**, parts of the empire generally worked together. Certainly the regiments raised in different regions supported each other on the battlefield. But as the war dragged on, problems grew.

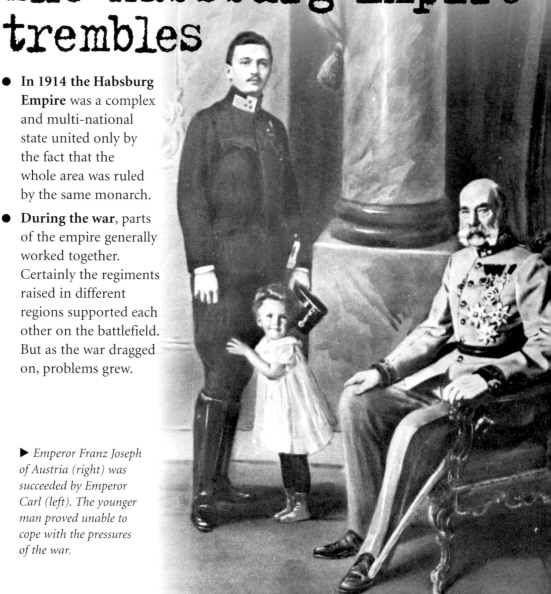

▶ *Emperor Franz Joseph of Austria (right) was succeeded by Emperor Carl (left). The younger man proved unable to cope with the pressures of the war.*

- **During the poor harvest of 1916**, the Hungarians refused to sell corn to other areas of the empire.

- **On 21 November 1916**, Emperor Franz Joseph died after reigning for 68 years. Many people in the empire began to wonder why they should remain loyal to the Habsburg Empire. They thought they might be better off with their own national states.

- **The new emperor**, Carl, was just 29 years old. He was intelligent and cared for his people, but had not been trained to be emperor as there had been two heirs in line before him.

- **In May 1917** Carl summoned the Imperial Parliament. He promised wide-ranging social and political reforms, but said they would have to wait until after the war.

- **When Lenin's Communist** revolution grabbed power in Russia, Carl began to fear a similar revolution in his lands.

- **Some of the regiments** freed by the surrender of Russia were moved to face the Italians or the Allied forces in Salonika. Others were positioned within the empire to guard against revolution.

- **By early 1918** the Habsburg Empire was running out of money. Emperor Carl was almost bankrupt.

... FASCINATING FACT ...

In Austria, Franz Joseph was emperor, in Hungary he was king and in Dalmatia he was duke. Each area also had its own local government, which cooperated with the central government.

Austria surrenders

- **During 1917**, the Czechs and Slovaks increasingly resented the fact that their wealthy industries were being taxed heavily to support the war effort. Led by Thomas Masaryk, they argued that the war was between Austria and Serbia, and had nothing to do with them.

- **In March 1918**, Masaryk persuaded the Allies to promise complete independence to a new country called Czechoslovakia after the war. Emperor Carl's idea of a federal state was no longer enough.

- **Masaryk began distributing** leaflets to Czech and Slovak regiments, urging them not to fight for the Austrians.

- **The Poles and Slavs** also set up secret organizations, but they were not as successful as Masaryk. Nevertheless, the Allies promised to support their claims to independence.

- **On 24 October 1918**, a massive Italian offensive, supported by British and French troops, took place on the river Piave front in northern Italy.

- **Italian General Armando Diaz** had 57 divisions and 7700 guns to assault the 52 divisions and 6000 guns of Austrian Archduke Joseph.

- **For several days** there was little movement. Then the town of Vittorio Veneto fell to the Italians on 30 October. Next day the town of Sacile was captured, along with bridges over the river Livenza.

▶ *A helmet perched on a rifle marks the grave of a British soldier. In the confusion of trench warfare, many men were hurriedly buried in unmarked graves – and thousands of them are still there.*

▶ *The British newspaper,* Daily Sketch, *celebrates the fact that Emperor Carl of Austria had announced he was breaking the alliance with Germany on 29 October 1918.*

- **On 3 November**, the Austrian army collapsed. Men threw away their guns and fled. Those that could not run fast enough, surrendered by the thousand to the Italians. In three days the Italians took 300,000 prisoners.

- **When news of the Battle of Vittorio Veneto** reached Emperor Carl, he lost his nerve. He wrote a letter that began, "Since I am filled by unchangeable love for all my nations, I will not place my person as an obstacle to their free evolution..."

- **The letter was taken** to be both an abdication of the crown and the dissolution of the empire. Austria was out of the war.

Bulgaria collapses

- **On 14 September 1918**, the Allied forces marching north from Salonika reached Bulgarian defences in the mountains north of the town. They pounded the defenders with artillery, then began an infantry attack.

- **On 15 September**, a 'Yugoslav' division attacked near Mount Vetrenik. The men were drawn from the southern Slav peoples who wanted freedom from the Austrian Empire.

- **On 16 September**, two Bulgarian regiments refused to attack, and discontent broke out elsewhere. Bulgarian General Lukov informed King Ferdinand that he thought the army would not fight much longer.

- **On 20 September**, Lukov ordered a general retreat. He began leading his men back to Bulgaria, abandoning the territories seized by King Ferdinand from Serbia. The Bulgarians were going home.

- **The Bulgarian Communists** led by Alexander Stamboliisky, declared that Bulgaria was a Soviet Republic on 27 September. He led 15,000 armed men towards Sofia. Bulgaria was now fighting a civil war.

- **On 29 September**, the retreating army of Lukov attacked the Communists, crushing the attempted revolution within hours.

- **The Communist leader**, Stamboliisky, fled. He abandoned Communism and became the democratically elected prime minister of Bulgaria.

> **...FASCINATING FACT...**
> When General Lukov told King Ferdinand that they were losing the war, the king shouted, "Go back to the front line and get killed."

▲ *A unit of Bulgarian infantry man the trenches near Uskub. In 1918 the Bulgarian army abandoned the front line and began marching home.*

- **On 30 September**, Lukov signed an armistice with the Allies. He agreed to hand over all heavy weapons, to allow Allied troops free movement through Bulgaria and to keep his men in barracks.

- **On 4 October**, King Ferdinand abdicated in favour of his son Boris III. Bulgaria was out of the war.

193

Turkey surrenders

▼ *The entry of the Arab horsemen of Prince Feisel into Damscus, Syria, in October 1918 marked the final collapse of Turkish resistance to the Allies.*

- **When the overwhelming** German attacks struck the British lines in France in the spring of 1918, all reserves and supplies were sent to hold the attacks.

- **In Palestine**, British General Allenby, guided by T E Lawrence, delayed his main offensive until September. In Mesopotamia, the Allied advance halted to await supplies.

- **On 17 September**, the assault on the Turks opened with an Arab raid on the town of Deraa. Lawrence utterly destroyed the rail junction, blocking all supplies from reaching the Turkish army in Palestine.

- **On 19 September**, Allenby attacked the Turks in the Jezreel Valley. Lacking supplies and demoralized, the Turks put up little fight. By 25 September, the Australian and New Zealand cavalry were in Amman.

- **The German commander** Liman von Sanders was so surprised by the British attack that he fled in his pyjamas.

- **On 27 September**, retreating Turks massacred over one hundred Arab women and children as revenge. Lawrence began to lose control over the Arabs.

- **A cavalry charge by Australian horsemen** defeated the Turks defending Damascus on 1 October – this turned out to be the last successful cavalry charge of modern warfare.

- **After the fall of Damascus**, the Turks effectively stopped fighting. A few desultory rearguard actions in Mesopotamia and Syria took place.

- **On 30 October**, Turkish diplomats boarded the British battleship *Agamemnon* to sign an armistice.

- **The Sultan was discredited** by the defeat and overthrown by General Mustafa Kemal, who was then elected as president of the new republic of Turkey in 1923. He radically modernized the government and economy.

Germany's 'Black Day'

- **On 18 July**, the French and Americans launched an attack to surround the Germans. General Ludendorff saw the trap and pulled his men back.

- **On 8 August**, a massive British–Canadian–Australian attack, led by 600 tanks, was launched on the German lines in front of Amiens.

- **At Amiens the German lines gave way**, allowing the Allies to advance 11 km by dusk. Thousands of men surrendered, many more fled to the east. Morale collapsed as six entire divisions gave up the fight.

- **When Ludendorff studied** the reports from Amiens he declared, "8 August was the Black Day of the German army." He lost hope of winning the war.

- **Ludendorff conferred** with Kaiser Wilhelm. They agreed that the war must end, but negotiations should only begin if Germany were doing well in a battle so that they could negotiate a favourable peace.

- **On 11 August**, Foch, the Allied commander in France, ordered the British to halt the attack at Amiens. German reserves were strengthening the line.

- **On 2 October**, the US 307th Regiment was surrounded by a German counter attack at Charlevaux. They held out until 7 October when an American attack reached them. Only 252 out of 700 men survived.

- **In October** a new government took over in Germany under Prince Max Scheidemann-Erzberger.

- **Prince Max sent a note** to US President Wilson asking for peace negotiations to begin.

▶ *Part of a large crowd of German soldiers captured at Amiens in August 1918. The collapse of morale proved to be catastrophic for Germany.*

...FASCINATING FACT...

On 8 October, Sergeant Alvin York reached the flank of a German battalion. In the next hour he killed 25 Germans, captured 135 more and cleaned out 35 machine guns posts.

Armistice in November

- **On 26 October**, German generals von Ludendorff and von Hindenburg met with Prince Max. They told him that the German army could hold out until the winter weather brought an end to Allied attacks.

- **Prince Max refused** to prolong the war. He fired Ludendorff and removed Hindenburg from all but purely ceremonial roles.

- **On 6 November**, the new supreme commander, General Groener, told the Kaiser that if they did not surrender within a week the army would collapse.

- **On 7 November**, Prince Max sent a delegation headed by Matthias Erzberger to agree an armistice. He asked the Allies to suspend fighting. French General Foch refused.

- **On 9 November**, representatives of Britain, France and the USA met the German delegation in a railway train parked in the Forest of Compiégne.

- **At 1 a.m. on 11 November** Prince Max replied that the German government agreed to the armistice terms. At 5 a.m. Erzberger signed the armistice. It stated that fighting would cease everywhere at 11 a.m.

- **On 10 November**, the British marched into the Belgian town of Mons, where they had first begun to fight more than four years earlier.

- **The same day**, a British air force pilot was shot down and badly wounded. His name was William Johns, later to become the author of the Biggles books.

- **On the night of 10 November** the statue of the Virgin Mary on top of Albert Cathedral, damaged by artillery fire in 1916, fell to the ground. Ever since it had been damaged, men believed that it would signal the end of the war.

- **The last man to be killed** was Canadian Private George Price, shot by a German sniper at 10.58 a.m. on 11 November.

▼ *When news of the armistice reached London, large crowds of cheering people formed and surged towards Buckingham Palace to begin peace celebrations.*

Talks at Versailles

- **On 18 January 1919**, the Peace Conference to agree the final terms, opened in Paris, in the Palace of Versailles. Representatives of all countries attended, as did many other groups and organizations.

- **The various delegations** came to Paris with differing aims and objectives, and with very different degrees of power and influence.

- **Germany, Turkey and Bulgaria were defeated countries** with little negotiating power. Their delegations hoped to limit the penalties imposed on their countries by the victors.

- **Russia had been defeated**, but now its Allies had won the war. The Russians wanted the Treaty of Brest-Litovsk cancelled and the return of all the lands that had belonged to the Tsar.

- **France had been invaded** by Germany twice in less than 50 years. The French wanted to impose conditions on Germany that would make a third invasion impossible. France also wanted the town of Alsace and Lorraine.

- **Belgium had been almost completely occupied** by Germany, but its army had fought on and had captured areas of German colonies in Africa. The Belgians wanted to regain their pre-war border in Europe and to gain the German colonies.

- **Britain wanted Germany** to pay for the damages inflicted during the war. Britain also hoped to take control of as much of the overseas German Empire as possible.

- **Italy wanted to gain** the Italian-speaking parts of the Habsburg Empire and hoped to gain control of the Dalmatian coast and Albania as well.

- **Austria, Hungary and other parts of the old Habsburg Empire** wanted to gain their independence, but not to be penalized for the actions of the empire during the war.

- **The USA wanted a peace settlement** that would make a new war in Europe unlikely. President Wilson thought the best way to achieve this was to set up an independent state for each nationality in Europe.

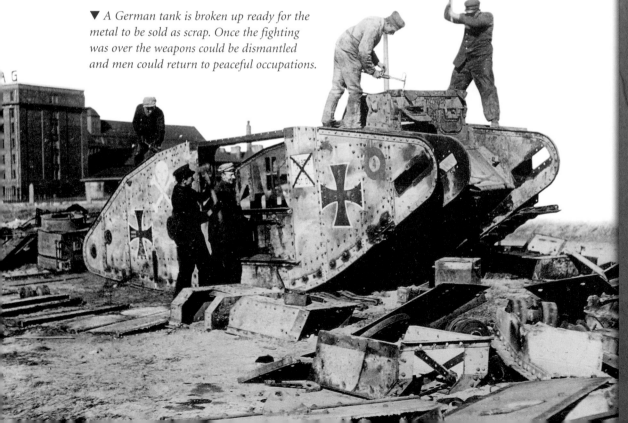

▼ *A German tank is broken up ready for the metal to be sold as scrap. Once the fighting was over the weapons could be dismantled and men could return to peaceful occupations.*

A new Europe

- **In June, the Treaty of Versailles** ending World War I was signed in the Palace of Versailles. Few countries got what they wanted – the victors got most.

- **Other treaties were signed** between smaller countries, known as the Versailles Settlement. The map of Europe was completely redrawn.

- **France gained** the towns of Alsace and Lorraine from Germany, while Belgium and Denmark also gained small border areas. Italy gained the Italian-speaking parts of the Habsburg Empire.

- **Serbia was merged** with the Slav-speaking areas of the old Habsburg Empire to form the new Yugoslavia. The Habsburg Empire was divided up into Austria, Hungary and Czechoslovakia. Romania gained Transylvania.

- **Poland was created** by joining the Polish-speaking areas of the former Russian, Habsburg and German empires.

- **Russia was given** back the Ukraine, but was forced to accept the independence of Finland, Estonia, Latvia and Lithuania.

- **Bulgaria lost small slices of territory** to Greece, Yugoslavia and Romania. Turkey retained only the lands that make up modern Turkey.

- **Several areas of Europe** were allowed to vote on which country they wished to join.

◀ The main talks at Versailles took place between politicians and soldiers of the victorious states. Each country wanted something different and the talks dragged on for months.

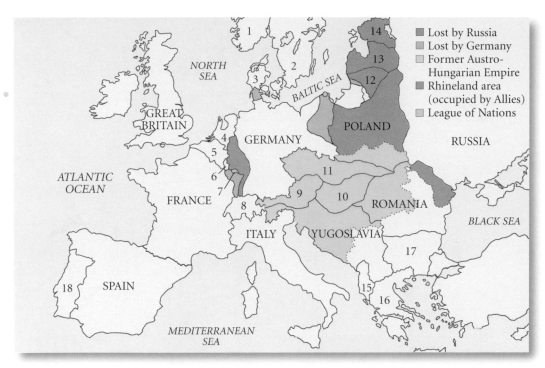

▲ *The Versailles Conference sought to satisfy the ambition of the smaller nations of Europe to achieve self-government, while respecting historic divisions and frontiers. The new face of Europe was destined to survive less than 20 years.*

KEY

1 Norway	10 Hungary
2 Sweden	11 Czechoslovakia
3 Denmark	12 Lithuania
4 Netherlands	13 Latvia
5 Belgium	14 Estonia
6 Luxembourg	15 Albania
7 Saarland	16 Greece
8 Switzerland	17 Bulgaria
9 Austria	18 Portugal

- **The Arabs were freed** from Turkish rule, but did not become fully independent. Iraq (Mesopotamia), Palestine and Jordan were put under British mandate. Syria and Lebanon went to a French mandate.

- **German colonies overseas were divided** up between Britain, Australia, Japan and France.

203

The League of Nations

- **The cost of World War I** was horrific for all involved. There was a widespread desire to avoid any future war. Nobody wanted to face such a terrible conflict again.

- **All countries had lost large** numbers of soldiers killed in battle, or dying of their wounds. Over eight million soldiers died.

- **US President Wilson suggested** that the countries of the world should join together to form a League of Nations that could ensure future peace.

- **The League of Nations** would be open to any country that wished to join. The members would pledge to work in friendship to solve any disputes.

- **If any country attacked** a member of the League, then all members of the League would mobilize their armed forces to impose a peaceful solution.

- **It was decided** that the League of Nations should be based in Switzerland. Large, luxurious offices and debating chambers were built in which the diplomats could meet.

- **A wave of optimism** swept the world that the Great War that had just ended was 'the war to end all wars'. It was hoped that the League of Nations would allow sensible people from each country to ensure world peace.

- **However, the League** had no method of enforcing any decisions it took. If a country chose to ignore the League, nothing could be done about it.

- **Some countries chose not to join** the League of Nations, even the USA.

- **For a while** the League of Nations worked well. However, new disputes arose that divided its members. Within 20 years it would be obsolete.

Military casualties

Germany	1,800,000
Russia	1,700,000
France	1,380,000
Austria	1,290,000
Britain	743,000
Italy	615,000
Romania	335,000
Turkey	325,000
Others	434,000

▲ *The numbers of military personnel killed during World War I was enormous. Although Germany lost more men than any other country, this represents 2.8 percent of its population, while France lost 3.5 percent and Russia almost 10 percent.*

Storing up trouble

- **US President Wilson wanted** the new borders to mark out areas where people of different nationalities lived. However, many areas had mixed populations that would not allow this. The Treaty of Versailles drew frontiers that left many people living in the 'wrong' country.

- **The borders of Poland** caused a particular problem. The Polish-speaking areas were large, but had no access to the sea that would allow trade with the rest of the world. Poland was therefore given the port of Danzig (Gdansk), which had a population 98 percent German.

- **Article 231 of the Treaty of Versailles stated** that the war had been caused by German aggression. The Germans believed that they had been responding to Russia's attack on Austria and deeply resented the clause.

- **Those countries deemed** to have attacked their neighbours were made to pay for damage caused (reparations). The bill for Germany was £24 billion – about £22,000 billion today. Bulgaria and Turkey were expected to pay less.

- **Germany was forbidden** from having an army of more than 100,000 men or more than six battleships. It was not allowed to have any submarines nor to have an air force of any type.

- **Many areas of eastern Europe** would suffer from unrest as people of different nationalities argued about rights in different areas.

> ### FASCINATING FACT
> The war was followed by a severe economic depression, caused partly by damage incurred during the war and partly by the reparations and other economic clauses of the Treaty of Versailles.

PEACE AND FUTURE CANNON FODDER

The Tiger: "Curious! I seem to hear a child weeping!"

▶ *A cartoon from 1919 predicts that war will return by 1940 – it proved to be an accurate prophecy.*

- **The Germans greatly resented** being blamed for the war, being forced to pay such vast reparations and losing so much territory.

- **In the 1920s and 1930s** the anomalies of the Treaty of Versailles were exploited by politicians eager to gain power.

- **In 1939 Nazi Germany**, led by Adolf Hitler, invaded Poland to regain Danzig and nearby areas. World War II had begun.

207

Index

Index

Index

Index

Index

Acknowledgements

The publishers would like to thank the following artists
whose work appears in this book:

Peter Dennis, Mike Saunders

Maps by Chris Moore

All artworks are from the Miles Kelly Artwork Bank

The publishers would like to thank the following picture sources
whose photographs appears in this book:

Page 21 John Frost Newspapers/ Page 22 Topfoto/ Page 25 www.pictorialpress.com/
Page 26 Topfoto/ Page 29 www.pictorialpress.com/ Page 35 Topfoto/ Page 36 Topfoto/
Page 38 Topfoto/ Page 41 John Frost Newspapers/ Page 45 www.pictorialpress.com/
Page 52 Topfoto/ Page 55 www.pictorialpress.com/ Page 58 Topfoto/
Page 61 www.pictorialpress.com/ Page 67 Topfoto/ Page 70 Topfoto/
Page 72 www.pictorialpress.com/ Page 77 www.pictorialpress.com/
Page 80 www.pictorialpress.com/ Page 83 Topfoto/ Page 95 www.pictorialpress.com/
Page 96 www.pictorialpress.com/ Page 101 Topfoto/ Page 107 Topfoto/
Page 109 John Frost Newspapers/ Page 114 Topfoto/ Page 117 www.pictorialpress.com/
Page 119 www.pictorialpress.com/ Page 120 www.pictorialpress.com/ Page 123 Topfoto/
Page 124 www.pictorialpress.com/ Page 131 John Frost Newspapers/
Page 132 www.pictorialpress.com/ Page 134 www.pictorialpress.com/ Page 136 Topfoto/
Page 139 Topfoto/ Page 140 www.pictorialpress.com/ Page 143 Topfoto/
Page 146 www.pictorialpress.com/ Page 151 Topfoto/ Page 152 Topfoto/
Page 155 Topfoto/ Page 159 www.pictorialpress.com/ Page 160 www.pictorialpress.com/
Page 162 Topfoto/ Page 165 www.pictorialpress.com/ Page 170 Topfoto/
Page 174 www.pictorialpress.com/ Page 177 Topfoto/ Page 180 Topfoto/
Page 183 www.pictorialpress.com/ Page 187 Topfoto/ Page 188 Topfoto/
Page 191 John Frost Newspapers/ Page 193 www.pictorialpress.com/ Page 194 Topfoto/
Page 197 www.pictorialpress.com/ Page 201 Topfoto/ Page 207 John Frost Newspapers

All other photographs are from:

Corel, ILN